Charle...

UNCEASING

A PARENT'S GUIDE TO CONQUER WORRY AND PRAY WITH POWER

SUSAN K MACIAS

To Charlene–

Thank you for all you have invested spiritually in my life. Love you!

Blessings–

Susan

UNCEASING A Parent's Guide to Conquer Worry and Pray with Power

Susan K. Macias

Click or visit: susankmacias.com

ISBN 978-0-9993085-0-9

CONTENTS

ACKNOWLEDGMENTS

Writing the pages of this book proved more difficult than I dreamed possible. The time, humility, honesty, and tears required were beyond what I could have imagined. From the moment I naively said, "I should write a book about all the Lord has taught me" to the moment I crawled across the finish line, my life has contained more self-doubt and desire to quit than I would like to admit.

The only reason I didn't quit is Jesus put people in my life to help me complete what God had begun.

The writers of Hill Country Christian Writers faithfully read and edited each chapter. Your input, wisdom, and writing skills pushed my own meager abilities along and made this a better manuscript.

Two of my writing friends pushed me even further. "Faithful are wounds of a friend" means you two friends were willing to give me tough advice and help me make tough cuts. Thanks for sticking with me, Sheri Hunt and Becky Seidschlag.

My parents, Jim and Diane Kleypas, are a constant source of encouragement and support. Your belief in me helped me keep going through immense self-doubt.

My seven beloved children: Caleb, Luke, Aaron, Grace, Leah, Hannah, and Abigail. Your grace, love, and willingness to put up with me gave my fingers strength to write. I quake thinking you will read words that reflect my best hope, while I recognize all the times I failed to live up to those ideals. I am sorry for when I worried, nagged, and reacted with frustration or anger. You walked through my learning of the lessons reflected here, and I appreciate your patience. You are infinitely worth every moment of prayer, and I promise to never stop praying for you.

My precious in-law children: Virginia, Misha, Giana, and Nathan. I am grateful my children chose so well, adding such lovely souls to our family. Thanks for willingly entering our crazy family. We are a richer group with you here.

My darling granddaughters: Olivia, Isabella, and Emiliana. As I prayed for your parents, I pledge to pray unceasingly that you will grow into magnificent daughters of the King. Your Daisy loves you very much.

My sweet Nathan, my parenting adventure buddy. You truly know the depth of my worrying heart. Thanks for loving me, encouraging me, editing my words, propping up my doubt, and walking beside me.

And Jesus—I hope I didn't misrepresent *any* of Your Words. They are life to my bones and oxygen to my lungs. I never want to miscommunicate them. Thanks for loving my children even more than I can imagine. I am confident that You will complete every single thing You have begun in them. I will be talking to You soon, because I have a few concerns we need to work on...

PART I

UNCEASING

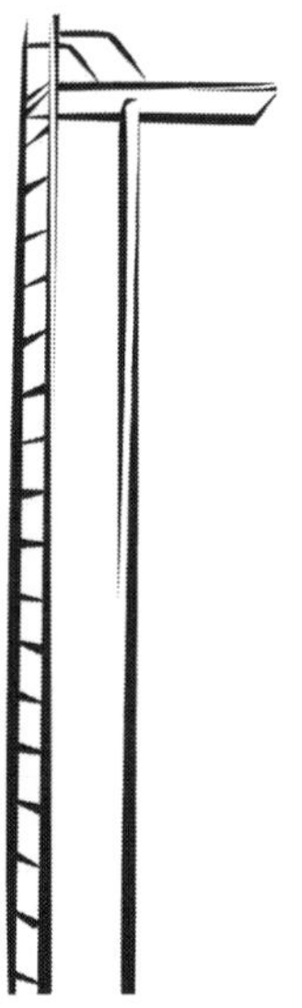

PREFACE

Hi, friend. I am so glad you found your way to this book. I am thinking you are a mom, because, after all, this is a parent's prayer guide, and in most cases, it is us moms who read books on this sort of thing. And I am guessing you have spent your fair share of time worrying about your kids, because that is what moms do, and usually we do it very well.

I am a champion worrier. And I want to admit right up front that I have not ACTUALLY conquered worrying. Yet. It might seem strange that I wrote a book about conquering worry when I haven't obtained complete victory in the battle, but it would be a silly waste of time if we had to wait around for me to beat worry into a bloody pulp before I shared the truth God has taught me about the power of prayer to conquer anxiety. He wants you and me to walk in confidence, and I fight alongside you to stay on that path.

I may not have conquered worry, but I now have an amazing weapon against it, and that is what I share in these pages. The truth tucked away in Philippians 1:3–11 has transformed my response to challenges in my children's lives. I pray that in these pages you also see the power in this passage and the truth that can free you to live in confidence that God is working in your kids' lives.

I also pray that you will be inspired to pray, pray often, and pray hard! I pray you will be *Unceasing* in your prayers. Our kids need us to be serious about our commitment to prayer in these days. My greatest motivation to write this book was that the kids of this generation (your children and mine) would be surrounded with the prayers of their parents. There is no more important thing we can do for our kids.

So, dive on in to *Unceasing*. At the end of each chapter are some Scriptures and prayers to help you get started praying. If you would like more suggestions, downloads, or encouragement, go to **http://www.susankmacias.com/unceasing** and sign up. You will find access there to resources to encourage and aid your prayer life.

I also invite you to the Facebook page **https://www.facebook.-com/unceasingprayerforkids/**. There we can encourage each other and pray for one another and our children. I look forward to meeting you.

May your heart overflow with thanksgiving and joy as you see Jesus more clearly, gain confidence in His good work in your child's heart, and pray for Him to fill your son or daughter with abounding love, knowledge and discernment, while producing fruit of righteousness to the glory of God.

Blessings- *Susan*

1

FIGHTING FOR MY KIDS

O you who hear prayer, to you shall all flesh come.

— Psalm 65:2

Moses surveyed the horizon from his hilltop perch. With apprehension clutching his heart, he turned and said to a messenger, "The armies of Amalek approach! Take word to Joshua. Prepare the army; the battle is near."

Standing behind Israel's leader, Aaron and Hur caught their breath. The advancing enemies appeared strong and ruthless. How could the Israelites, weary from their wanderings and previous battles, defeat such a foe?

"What is the plan, Moses?" Aaron asked. Now old men, Moses, Aaron, and Hur were not of much use on the battlefield. Instead, they stood on the hilltop to oversee the military engagement that would soon begin.

Silent for a moment, Moses examined the rod clutched in his hands. "When Yahweh called me to lead our people out from bondage in Egypt, I doubted I could succeed. I am ashamed to say I argued with God, even reminding Him of my weaknesses. But from the burning bush, Yahweh asked, 'What is in your hand?'

"This..." Moses extended the rod, "This staff was what I held. Through our entire struggle, our God has used this simple shepherd's staff to do many amazing acts."

Aaron and Hur smiled at the memories. Years before, Moses had lifted that same rod over the Red Sea, resulting in the waters parting in the most extraordinary miracle they had ever experienced. And just a few days ago Moses had struck a rock with the rod in this parched land and water poured out for the people.

"I still am not sure why God chose to use me, as well as you two," grinned Moses at his brother and friend. "But He called us to be faithful and obey Him, and trust Him with the outcome. So here we stand again, in an impossible situation where we must do what Yahweh says and watch Him work."

As the sounds of impending battle reached the three men's ears, they peered down.

"Our God will do something amazing again," Moses proclaimed. Facing the battle, Moses confidently raised the staff of God above his head.

As Moses stood, arms stretched high, the three men observed the clash below them. "Look!" cried Aaron, "Our army seems to prevail. There is hope!"

But as the battle raged on, Moses faltered. His arms wearied; his back ached. He could hold his arms up no longer. When he lowered the rod, however, they witnessed a visible change on the battlefield. Amalek began to push back and gain the upper hand.

"Moses, you must raise the rod again, or we will be defeated," Hur urged.

Moses raised the rod, and Israel rallied. But again he tired, the rod lowered, and the Amalekite army surged.

"I am weary, friends. How will we win this battle when I have no strength to continue?" Moses asked.

Aaron and Hur took one look at each other and immediately went to work. Hur dragged a rock near so that Moses could sit. Aaron aided his brother to sit and positioned the staff in Moses's weary hands. Together they raised his arms and remained at Moses's side, sustaining their exhausted leader. They held him. He held the rod. And the Israelites defeated their enemy!

Parenting and Prayer

Parenting. Not only the hardest job on the planet but also one of the most rewarding. I remember staring into the eyes of my first newborn baby. Overwhelmed by a love that started from my toes and flowed to every pore, I knew I would do anything to help this soul live, develop, and thrive. As each subsequent child entered our family, I continued to make the same divine pact. I willingly sacrificed vast quantities of time, money, and energy throughout their childhoods. I did so gladly.

My husband and I planned our children's education, protected their health, provided opportunities, and attended to their needs. All of those investments were wise and good. But while important in their temporal dimensions, they held no guarantee of eternal effects.

Eventually I discovered that of all the jobs where I invested my time and energy as a parent, nothing was more important than prayer. Nothing! Yet even knowing that, I felt tension. How could I both do enough for my children AND pray enough for them?

Just as Moses stood in the gap for his people when they fought the

Amalekites, I needed to do the same for my kids. However, throughout the twenty-nine years my husband and I have been parents, I confess I found it easier to spend more time fretting than praying, nagging than crying out to the Lord, and worrying than standing with the rod of God over my head.

As I tried to pray more, I felt hindered by a personal tendency to worry and a bad habit of trying to direct God. I needed to learn how to pray powerfully for my children. I yearned for a framework that would direct me toward the effective prayer life I craved.

One day, reading the first chapter of Philippians, I realized that this was it. Philippians 1:3–11 encapsulated my parent's heart. I began to use it as a guide for my prayers. But a funny thing happened on the way to the prayer closet. This Scripture not only helped me to pray, but it also pierced and judged the thoughts and intentions of my heart (see Hebrews 4:12). And through that painful, profitable process, this passage not only taught me *what* to pray, it also trained my attitude and emotions *while* I was praying.

Following Philippians 1:3–11 changed how I viewed prayer. It also revealed to me the power prayer contains. Prayer is the only vehicle that has ever delivered peace or joy in the midst of trouble. Does that sound like something you want to learn, too? Then let's take a closer look at prayer.

What Prayer Is Not

When Moses stood with his arms raised high, holding the rod of God, it might have appeared he was not doing much of anything. Yet, the success or failure of the battle rested more in his stalwart stillness than in all the activity on the battlefield.

Prayer often feels like I am DOING nothing. Maybe it is more comforting to DO for my children than to simply pray, because my actions, investments, or admonishments give me a false sense of security. My works "prove" I am a good parent (or at least trying to be) in spite of my fears to the contrary. If I DO all I can, I will have better results. Right?

But prayers? Speaking my heart inaudibly. And then waiting. And waiting. And hoping God will act. In the moment, it can feel like I accomplish nothing at all.

I admit, in the past I often used prayer as a fallback after trying all other options. I pulled it out every now and then, when I was desperate enough, yet all the while not quite confident of God's ability to act.

In difficult or troublesome times, when I had no apparent ability to affect an outcome, worrying was the one thing I felt I COULD do. But God commands, in Matthew 6:34, "Do not worry..." Here, God leaves no wiggle room to justify anxiety.

Maybe the Lord is so adamant about not worrying because He knows the negative effects it causes. He created my body with the ability to physically respond to crisis by producing cortisol and adrenaline. Continual worry keeps my body in this stress mode. When I anxiously take on the responsibility of actions outside of my control, I put my body in a constant state of tension that I cannot sustain without doing damage to myself.

This tension produces lovely effects like weight gain, high cholesterol and blood pressure, poor sleep, and depression. My stomach aches, my muscles tighten, I think poorly, and my head hurts. God doesn't want me to live like that. Proverbs 12:25 states, "Anxiety in a man's heart weighs him down." Worry produces anxiety, which weighs down my heart and steals my joy. God loves me too extravagantly to let me walk around with a heavy heart. His design has always been for me to place my concerns in His ever-capable hands.

In Philippians 4:6–7, I am commanded, "...do not be anxious about anything, but in everything by prayer and supplication with thanksgiving let your requests be made known to God. And the peace of God, which surpasses all understanding, will guard your hearts and your minds in Christ Jesus." Reread that last sentence: "the peace of God, which surpasses all understanding, will guard your hearts and your minds in Christ Jesus."

I need God's peace guarding my heart and my mind. They are the battlegrounds where I alternate between prayer and fear.

Fretting carries the responsibility of problems and concerns. Prayer transfers the weight from my weak, burdened heart to the shoulders of the only One who is strong enough to handle it.

Worry makes me feel like I am doing something. Prayer actually does something.

Have you ever read the book, *If You Give a Mouse a Cookie*? It is a classic tale of how wanting one thing leads to desiring another and then another. Someday I may write a book called *If You Give a Mom a Worry*. If there is a concern, whether valid or not, that I have about my child's life, I usually fall prey to worry. As I worry, I start to imagine the next possible negative thing that could happen. And then the next possible issue. And the one after that...

The next step is worse. I begin worrying about those potential problems. Did you catch that? I start to worry about things that are not actually happening. I worry over things that MIGHT happen.

The Bible has a term for the things I imagine that are not based in fact: "vain...imagination" or "futile...thinking." Romans 1:21 states, "For although they knew God they did not honor Him as God or give thanks to him, but *they became futile in their thinking* and their foolish hearts were darkened" [emphasis added].

Talk about a joy slayer. With plenty of actual items of concern in my life, I don't need to imagine my worst nightmare. But how do I break the cycle of endless worry? That, my friend, is where prayer comes in.

As I struggled to become a prayer warrior, the Lord revealed to me many false assumptions I held about prayer. For instance, I learned prayer is not a desperate cry that doubts the possibility of results. Nor is it a laundry list of complaints, or a three-point action plan that I am looking for God to rubber stamp.

So, if prayer is not a magic bottle that I rub every day so the genie will pop out and give me what I want, what is it?

I am so glad you asked.

What Prayer Is

Be anxious for nothing. Pray for everything. That sums up God's command in Philippians 4:6–7.

While this is a simple command, it is not easy for us to come to prayer first. Oswald Chambers said, "We tend to use prayer as a last resort, but God wants it to be our first line of defense. We pray when there's nothing else we can do, but God wants us to pray before we do anything at all."

Colossians 4:2 calls us to be devoted to prayer, and according to Strong's Concordance, this kind of devotion involves steadfast, unremitting, continual perseverance and courage.[3] Being devoted to prayer means I am not praying once for a situation and then walking away. Instead it means I stick with it, praying over and over, believing God will act.

Does that sound like hard work? That is because it is! Paul tells us that Epaphras "labors earnestly in prayer" for the believers in Colossae. The picture of this labor is one of struggle, contention, and fighting with adversaries.[4] In fact, this type of active, strenuous prayer requires so much energy and concentration there is little time left to waste in worrying.

Although I long desired to cultivate this type of devoted prayer in my life as a parent, I found myself sliding back into anxiety and complaint. Philippians 1:3–11 helped me out of that pit. Sometimes I would pray through all the verses, but other times I would camp out on one particular request, depending upon the need of the moment.

Philippians 1 is not magic. It is not a mantra that if repeated often enough will have a guaranteed result. But it contains the inspired, infallible Word of God and it records Paul's actual prayers for his "children" in clear language that we can still use today. My children are my most important disciples, whom my heart yearns to see walk in spiritual maturity. So, I employ Paul's prayers and thoughts toward his small church as a guide to my intentional prayer toward my own "small church."

But, let me be honest with you. Praying through these verses has taught me hard lessons about the purpose and practice of prayer.

Prayer is not about getting God's heart lined up with mine. Instead, prayer involves getting my heart lined up with God's.

Prayer lays my own dreams and plans for my children down at the feet of the loving Father of the universe and asks for His best in their lives.

Prayer requires trust in the invisible Hand of God. It stands in faith and rests in hope.

Prayer means I believe God will act in ways not yet seen[5] and maybe not even yet imagined.[6]

Prayer demands the humility to believe that God can do far more than I ever could in my child's life.

Prayer talks to God about my children instead of nagging my children about God.

Prayer speaks God's truth and promises personally OVER my child, not TO my child.

And ultimately, prayer focuses very little on me, my children, and our problems. Prayer focuses on the Mover and Maker of our lives.

Prayer is about God.

Prayer unleashes the power of the Lord in my family more than any other action. It overrides my failures. It surpasses my children's weaknesses. It is not limited by my strength or my children's strength. Rather, it taps into the ultimate strength of the universe—the Lord's strength.

Like all significant work, prayer requires heart and involves sacrifice. It demands time, the parental commodity with the highest demand and lowest quantity. 1 Thessalonians 5:17 commands believers to "pray without ceasing," which means that in God's economy prayer is not only vital, it must be continual. The supreme challenge is to pray, to pray effectively, and to pray unceasingly.

Like Moses, I stand in the gap for my kids. I don't have a literal staff of the Lord to hold high while they struggle in battle. But I do have a figurative one. I have prayer.

But just like Moses experienced when he held up the rod, I can grow weary during the long fight and struggle to keep praying. At those times, Philippians 1:3–11 is my "Aaron and Hur," lifting my arms so I can continue. I pray you find that same encouragement tucked away in the pages of this book.

How to Use This Book

This book is a result of the Lord tutoring me for years through this passage in Philippians.

Following the verses of Philippians 1:3–11, there are three sections in this book: Platform, Position, and Petition.

- **Platform** looks at Philippians 1:3–5 and deals with the heart, the seedbed of not only faith but also worry. Getting my emotions in line with my faith changed my parental stress

level more than any other thing I ever tried. And it rocked my prayer life too!
- **Position** examines Philippians 1:6–8 and gives feet to faith and a foundation to resolve. To walk in assurance as a mom, I learned I needed to trust Jesus more. Realizing that the ONLY thing I needed confidence in was God set this captive free.
- **Petition** lays out *what* to pray based on Philippians 1:9–11. While this may be the only part you were looking for, don't skip ahead! The heart and mind shift found in the first two sections are where the joy and freedom can be found. *I believe God wants to release parents to experience great satisfaction in Him, even when our children struggle.*

Each chapter is followed by questions to help you apply what you learn.

There are also prayer guides after each chapter. These have Scripture that apply to the specific topic discussed, and then a sample prayer to demonstrate how to pray God's Word right back to Him. I hope you find them useful to launch your prayer life to the stratosphere.

Let's Get Started!

Want to pray for your child's spiritual maturity and ultimate success? What better place to start than with the heart of God, His Word! As you use these Scriptures to guide your prayer life, I pray that you will walk away from worry and into the freedom of confidence in God working His mighty plan in your child's life.

> Satan does not care how many people read about prayer if only he can keep them from praying.[7]
>
> — Paul E. Billheimer

Fear not, for I am with you;
be not dismayed, for I am your God;
I will strengthen you, I will help you,
I will uphold you with my righteous right hand.

— Isaiah 41:10, ESV

PART II

THE PLATFORM

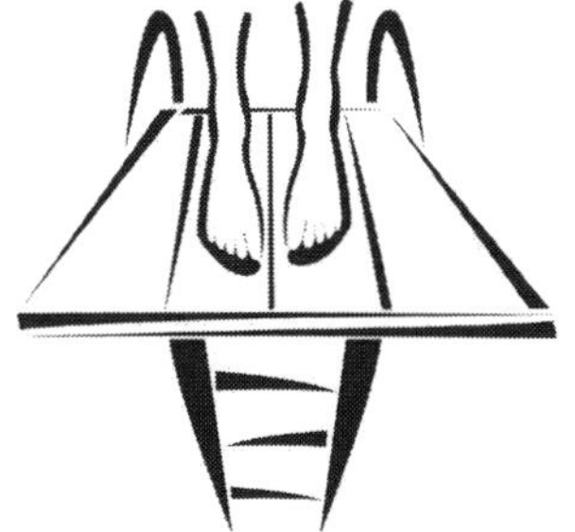

THE PLATFORM OF PRAYER

I thank my God every time I remember you.
I always pray with joy in my every prayer for all of you because of your participation in the gospel from the first day until now.

— PHILIPPIANS 1:3–5

I remember the summer I finally conquered the high dive at our neighborhood pool. It was only a ten-foot-high board, but to a scrawny, ten-year-old girl, it seemed one hundred feet from the water. I had climbed the ladder and crept to the end of the board a few times, but I could never overcome my instinct of self-preservation. Each time I chickened out and took the humiliating climb back down the ladder. The older boys waiting in line to dive sneered as I passed. They could; they had already overcome their fear.

But finally, a day came when I was resolute. This time would be different. Nervously, I ascended the ladder and crept out to the end, determined that the only way I was going down was into the water. With knees shaking and heart beating, my common sense discouragingly whispered, "*This is a horrible idea. It would be better to endure sneers from the boys than a ten-foot belly flop!*" Ignoring the voice in my head, I took one tentative step off the end of the board. After falling forever, my body cut through the water, straight into the deep end. When I bobbed back up without injury, my pride and confidence swelled. I might as well have walked through fire.

In reality, it wasn't the water that scared me, but the platform. The ten-foot platform was scary high in my childlike mind. But I needed to conquer the platform to accomplish the dive.

To this day, I love watching diving competitions in the Olympics. The platform for the high dive is thirty-three feet, over three times that of my childhood adventure. It amazes me how anyone could overcome their fear, not only enough to leap off that height but enough to perform flips and twists on the way down. Yet it is the height of the platform that allows for the accomplishment. You can't have one without the other.

The Prayer Platform

If I am not careful, I treat prayer like my first attempts at high-diving. I tentatively inch my way toward the end of the prayer diving board, hoping my bravado overcomes my quaking heart.

Honestly, deciding to dive into prayer, instead of wading through prayer, is scarier than diving from ten feet up. It is more like the thirty-three-foot-platform-diving kind of scary. I must say "no" to the fear that I will belly flop in my prayers. That they won't be heard. That I will waste my time. That my words will never go higher than the ceiling.

I have to ignore "common sense" that tells me to do something rather than to waste time asking God to do something. I have to reject the sneers of those who "know better" than putting their hope in prayers.

I must take the leap of faith that puts all my hope in God and His work in my kids' lives and become an Olympic-level prayer athlete for my children.

But what is the right platform from which to take my dive into prayer? It is stated perfectly in Philippians 1:3–5. There are three planks to this platform:

- Being thankful
- Feeling joyful
- Seeing correctly

All three planks are necessary. All three require a concerted act of the will to be successfully integrated into my prayer life. They are the place I have to start, and they drastically change not only how I pray but also what I pray. The same holds true for you. In the next three chapters, we learn how to build this platform and radically change our prayer life.

So, are you ready? Then climb the ladder to the high dive, boldly step out to the edge, and courageously take the plunge into God's power, grace, provision, work, and redemption through crazy, abandoned, confident prayer! It is better than walking through fire. You will never be the same.

> We must begin to believe that God, in the mystery of prayer, has entrusted us with a force that can move the Heavenly world, and can bring its power down to earth.[8]
>
> — Andrew Murray

Every time you cross my mind, I break out in exclamations of thanks to God. Each exclamation is a trigger to prayer. I find myself praying for you with a glad heart. I am so pleased that you have continued on in this with us, believing and proclaiming God's Message, from the day you heard it right up to the present.

— Philippians 1:3–5, The Message

2

I THANK GOD ALWAYS

Scripture:
I thank my God in all my remembrance of you.
(Philippians 1:3)
Prayer:
Thank You, Lord, for my children.

Steam rose from my coffee cup, which sat beside my open Bible and journal, all waiting for me to participate in my morning quiet time. But I stared out the window instead, dread surrounding my heart. I could neither read nor drink, and could barely manage a groan of a prayer.

This despair existed because my twenty-two-year-old son, at that very moment, was traveling alone, on a motorcycle, down a desolate highway. After a cataclysmic personal crisis, he decided a bit of adventure was just the ticket. So, he jumped on his motorcycle and began traveling from South Texas to northern Colorado. By himself.

Now on the second day of his big adventure, he traveled across the desolate plains of West Texas. Did I mention he was on a motorcycle? Alone? On a highway? If justification to worry ever existed, it was now.

A number of potentially disastrous scenarios danced through my mind and mocked my faith. My thoughts reeled at the dangers he faced.

As I sat powerless to keep him safe, I faced a decision—worry or pray? The obvious answer to every mother is BOTH, of course!

My tendency toward anxiety always hampered my prayers. But today, if I wanted to pray with power for my son, I had to stop wringing my hands. I also needed to stop imagining him wrecked on the side of the road. That picture in my head only produced fretting.

I had to start from a different platform entirely. The choice was mine. My eyes fluttered across my open Bible and landed on Philippians 4:6. There I discovered the light that could help me escape the tunnel of despair, where I was currently trapped. This verse proclaimed, "*Do not be anxious about anything,* but in everything by prayer and supplication *with thanksgiving* let your requests be made known to God" (Philippians 4:6, ESV, emphasis added).

At first, I felt an argument rising inside: "Lord, how am I honestly not supposed to be anxious? I am so worried I can barely breathe. Don't You realize how much danger he is in?" (Don't you just love that? I wondered if the omniscient God KNEW how much danger my son was in?!)

Then I zeroed in on the words, "with thanksgiving."

"Lord! With thanksgiving? Are you kidding? You want me to give thanks for this?"

Reassurance from the Holy Spirit confirmed that yes, this impossible platform of thankfulness was where I needed to start. Ignoring the resistance of my common sense, I dared myself to believe the

Word. And even though it ran counter to everything I felt, I started with thanksgiving.

"Thank You, God, for my son. Thank You that he is never out of Your sight or beyond Your reach. Lord, he is so broken and sad. Please use this time on the road to expand his vision of You, so that he would trust You more. Thank You that You love him so much."

Starting with thanksgiving began to transform my attitude. Over the three-day trip, Jesus and I spent lots of time together, during which I made an effort to start with gratitude. I later learned those prayers were important, such as the time he broke down on the side of a highway and a random trucker helped him get his motorcycle to a small town. Or when he rode through a near-blinding snow storm while eighteen-wheelers zoomed past.

The entire time I was thanking the Lord for my son, God was busy protecting and sustaining him.

> The very act of praise releases the power of God into a set of circumstances and enables God to change them if this is His design... I have come to believe that the prayer of praise is the highest form of communication with God, and one that always releases a great deal of power into our lives.[9]
>
> — Merlin R. Carothers

Diagnosis: Worry

With my children, I continually face impossible situations where I am powerless to make things right. So, I must use the only tool at my disposal: prayer. As I learned with my son's trip, beginning with thankfulness is the way I avoid the worry that hinders my prayer.

Worry crowds out joy. But thanksgiving crowds out worry.

Anxiety and fear paralyze me as a mom. I possess the remarkable talent of magnifying potential problems and constructing every horrible scenario possible.

I imagined my son being thrown from his bike, landing in a ditch, with no one to help him. Or maybe he was being beaten and robbed and left for dead. Or maybe...

Lamentations 3:23 promises that God's mercies are new every morning. But those mercies are available for reality—not for what I imagine in my head.

Romans 1:21 warns us that "... although they knew God they did not honor Him as God or give thanks to him, but *they became futile in their thinking* and their foolish hearts were darkened" (emphasis added). The people Paul describes here had two basic choices: honoring and thanking God, or succumbing to futile thoughts.

As my son sped across West Texas on his motorcycle, I was subject to the same choice. When I chose wrongly, I experienced the same demise: wrong thinking and a darkened heart. I fell victim to my mind's speculations, and my prayers were powerless.

But when I kept my focus laser-trained on Jesus, I could obey His command to not be fearful about ANYTHING. Instead of fretting, I could thank the Lord for my son and His plan for him and then let Him know my request that he survive.

Philippians 4:6a is a command, "Be anxious for nothing."

Let me repeat that—be anxious for nothing. NOTHING. Zilcho. Nada. Nyet.

When I decide to do something else with my concerns for my children, new prayer possibilities arise. I have the opportunity to obey Philippians 4:6b, "...but in everything by prayer and supplication with thanksgiving let your requests be made known to God." (NASB)

Many of my challenges as a parent result from anxiety. But God's imperative wording in Philippians 4:6 commands me to not be anxious, but to pray with thanksgiving.

This is why we give thanks as we begin unceasing prayer. The very first thing Paul prays in Philippians 1:3 is thanksgiving: I **thank** my God in all my remembrance of you.

If I ignore the command to not be anxious, and if I neglect to pour out my heart in grateful, joyful prayer, then I am susceptible to all kinds of negative and destructive actions. I nag, prod, remind, and badger. I don't know about your experience, but those never produced godliness or good decisions in my kids! Trust me, I tried them. They don't work. In fact, they usually cause my children to run the other way.

Lack of gratitude and anxiety also produce some other ugly tendencies in me. I compare my family to others who I assume are doing a better job (at least according to their Facebook posts and pictures). I allow sleep-depriving thoughts to rob me of rest. I condemn myself or my husband for past parenting mistakes that might be the cause of the current crisis. Or I give destructive emotions like blame, guilt, hopelessness, sorrow, and despair license to run amok in my heart.

No wonder God is so clear! Isn't God good as He both diagnoses the problem and prescribes the antidote?

- **Diagnosis:** I am worrying.
- **Prescription:** I need to pray with thanksgiving (see Philippians 1:3).
- **Prognosis:** I will gain the peace of God, which will guard my heart and my mind (see Philippians 4:7).

That prognosis results in the complete cure for fear; peace is the polar opposite emotion to fear. My mind and heart are the seedbeds for all this worry and anxiety. They are where I need a guard—a big, strong, iron-clad guard. And what better guard could there be than the Creator and Sustainer of the universe?

> Worry implies that we don't quite trust God is big enough, powerful enough, or loving enough to take care of what's happening in our lives.
>
> Stress says the things we are involved in are important enough to merit our impatience, our lack of grace towards others, or our tight grip of control.
>
> Basically, these two behaviors communicate that it's okay to sin and not trust God because the stuff in my life is somehow exceptional.[10]
>
> — Francis Chan

Warning: It Is Hard!

God clearly commands me to be thankful in order to guard myself from the worry that easily entangles me. So, I will be thankful. All the time. No matter what.

Right?

The reality is that the times I feel anxious are the times I have difficulty being thankful. My children face real-world problems. They make poor choices. They experience failure or opposition. In challenging or painful situations, thankfulness scarcely seems a reasonable response.

When I look at my kids only through the lens of my concerns or their bad choices, I have a hard time seeing anything to appreciate. I am blinded to the gifts and provisions for which I could be grateful.

Consider what Paul says to the Corinthians, a group of believers doing all sorts of things wrong. This church had spiritual, moral, and relational problems. Paul scolds and corrects them throughout all fifteen chapters of First Corinthians.

But Paul declares, at the beginning of the letter, in 1 Corinthians 1:4, "*I thank my God always* concerning you" (emphasis added).

Paul starts with thanksgiving.

He ALWAYS thanks God for the Corinthians.

This principle occurs again in Ephesians where Paul tells this early church that he does "*...not cease giving thanks* for you, while making mention of you in my prayers" (Ephesians 1:16, NASB, emphasis added). Even though he also took issue with errors that had crept into their church, unceasing thanksgiving permeated his prayer for them.

Prayer rooted in gratitude leads directly to joy, the next plank in our platform. So even when I am not crystal clear about what to be thankful for, I still need to always give thanks without ceasing.

When times are challenging, thankfulness is unfortunately not my go-to emotion. Which means, if I don't REMEMBER to be thankful, I quickly devolve into becoming a complainer, and a comparer, and an unsatisfied, unhappy wanter of something different.

Starting my prayers in Philippians 1:3 and being thankful when my circumstances stink requires an act of the will. The best way to remember to be thankful is to intentionally remember how God moved in the past. Then I can confidently pray for Him to move in the future.

Jesus Did It

Our Savior provided the best examples of thankfulness. In his gospel, Matthew uses the same Greek word for "thanks" as Paul uses in Philippians when Jesus gives thanks, *eucharisteo*.

The first example of *eucharisteo* is in Matthew 15:36, when Jesus took seven loaves of bread and a few fish and, illogically, according to our limited human understanding, assumed they would be enough to feed a large crowd of thousands.

The disciples were incredulous, but Jesus, "took the seven loaves and the fish; and *giving thanks*, He broke them and started giving them to the disciples, and the disciples gave them to the people. And they all ate and were satisfied, and they picked up what was left over of the broken pieces, seven large baskets full" (Matthew 15:36–37, NASB, emphasis added).

Jesus took the small, insufficient supply of food and through thanksgiving produced excess. Abundance. Overflow.

Is your energy for prayer low?

Is your faith for prayer weak?

Is your doubt and fear for your children strong?

Are you incredulous that Christ is doing anything in their lives or that your child will even let Him work?

Take the meager supplies that are left in your weary heart and GIVE THANKS, *eucharisteo*. Then watch in amazement as the God of multiplying grace increases your prayers and your faith.

Jesus Did It Again

The last recorded event of Christ offering thanks is when He gathered with His disciples in the Upper Room.

As Judas left the room, an uncomfortable hush fell. Could it be that Judas would betray their Rabbi? The events of the last few days crowded their minds as the disciples tried to make sense of it all.

Lazarus had been raised from the dead. The entry of Jesus into Jerusalem for Passover had been met with crowds cheering and waving palms. At the same time, rumors of plots against Jesus's life swirled on the edges of conversations. Even Jesus Himself spoke of His betrayal and death.

What could it all mean?

And now one of their own had left them in a cloud of dark mystery. Yet, through all this upheaval, Jesus remained calm and resolute.

As the Passover meal began, the disciples tried to get ahold of themselves. They had celebrated this feast every year of their lives, but this Passover seemed very different.

Gathered around the table, the remaining eleven disciples gazed at Jesus. He took the bread, gave a blessing, broke it, and passed it around, saying, "Take, eat; this is my body" (Matthew 26:26b).

Next, He took the cup, "and *when he had given thanks* he gave it to them, saying, 'Drink of it, all of you, for this is my blood of the covenant, which is poured out for many for the forgiveness of sins'" (Matthew 26:27–28, emphasis added).

The bread was His body? The wine His blood? What could that mean?

Over the next few hours, the disciples' lives were turned upside down. They witnessed their Rabbi arrested, beaten, accused, and condemned. Then, in horrified numbness, they watched Him be crucified.

As the blood poured from His side, maybe one of them remembered the evening before. Jesus had said the cup was the blood of the covenant, poured out for them. Representing Jesus's suffering and spilled blood, that Passover cup was exactly the cup for which Jesus had given thanks, *eucharisteo*.

As a believer, I know the rest of the story. Jesus suffered and died for me and for all who come to Him. In the process, He defeated death and Hell, and paid for every sin I have ever committed or will ever commit. He redeemed my life and now calls me to follow Him. He saves me.

That salvation does not start in some distant heaven. It begins now. It applies to every situation and relationship I have.

Jesus offered thanks over the cup of suffering because by it He would defeat the enemy and provide a way for His people.

If Jesus began with thanksgiving when faced with crucifixion, then I have no excuse to not begin with the same. Nothing my children or I face is so bad I get a pass on this. I must start with thankfulness.

Does that sound impossible? Well, keep reading. The Lord has a plan to help us. To be thankful, we must remember.

Remember to Remember!

Are you in the middle of suffering? Does the road ahead of you and your child look dark and terrifying? Are you facing a situation that only the God of grace can transform and redeem?

The Word reminds me to, "*Recall* the miraculous deeds He performed, His mighty acts and the judgments He decreed" (Psalm 105:5, emphasis added).

I have to be reminded to remember, because I so easily forget.

I forget all God orchestrated already. I forget how He protected. I forget how He provided. I forget how He led. I forget how He loved.

When forgetful, I can NEVER be thankful or hopeful. But through recalling and reminiscing and recollecting, I begin to scratch the surface of the magnitude of all God orchestrates for me and for those I love. Once the idea of that glory dawns upon me, I have no choice but to sing forth praises to the only One who deserves praise, no matter the circumstances.

Take a minute and REMEMBER:

- God is good and His love endures for generations. (see Psalm 136:1,2)
- He has engraved your child in the palm of His hand. (see Isaiah 49:14,16)
- He has protected your child and keeps his or her soul. (see Psalm 121:7)
- He will never leave your child or forsake him or her. (see Deuteronomy 31:6)

Give thanks!

BE THANKFUL!

Over and over again.

Don't forget the rest of the story! When situations are at their bleakest, Jesus is nowhere close to being finished. Take the worst-case scenario, lay it on the altar, and GIVE THANKS. *All circumstances that require divine intervention, complete transformation, and supernatural infusion demand thanksgiving.*

Are you ready to be a parental prayer warrior?

Then start with thanksgiving.

> ***I will remember the works of the Lord. Yes, I will remember the amazing things you did long ago!***
>
> — Psalm 77:11, NIV

PRINCIPLE:

When my thanksgiving is unceasing, my worry decreases and my prayers will multiply.

APPLICATION

Scripture: I thank my God in all my remembrance of you. (Philippians 1:3, ESV)

Prayer: Thank You, Lord, for my children.

- Spend some time with Philippians 1:3 and just thank the Lord for you children.

Philippians 4:6a is a command: "Be anxious for nothing." What prevents you from not being anxious about anything?

Are there some things for which it feels impossible to give thanks? Why? I encourage you to do it anyway! List them below and then spend time thanking God for each one and for what He is going to do.

List every item you can recall that worries you. Identifying them in black and white helps reduce their power over you. Give every single one to Jesus in prayer.

Now list anything you are thankful for. It doesn't need to be big, just list every item that comes to mind. The more you write, the more that will come to mind. You might want to start a journal of thankfulness.

Last, list every attribute of God you can recall. Then take a moment and spend time thanking the Lord for *who* He is. We have to recognize and believe in His ability in our kids' lives in order to move away from worry.

Prayers of Thanksgiving

Each of the following Scriptures proclaims thankfulness. Following each verse is a sample prayer showing how to use the truth to offer a prayer back to the Lord. There is room for you to write your own thoughts or prayers down.

(More Scripture and prayers can be found at **http://www.susankmacias.com/unceasing**)

- Psalm 107:22. NASB: Let them also offer sacrifices of thanksgiving, and tell of His works with joyful singing.
- Lord, I am so worried about my child today that to offer thanksgiving is a sacrifice. But since You ask me to do just that, I will thank You. Thank You for my child, thank You that You are at work, thank You that nothing is hidden from You. Help me sing to You today with joy.

- Isaiah 51:3: For the LORD comforts Zion; he comforts all her waste places and makes her wilderness like Eden, her desert like the garden of the LORD; joy and gladness will be found in her, thanksgiving and the voice of song.
- Today, Jesus, my heart feels like a desert and my mind like a waste place. Thank You that You restore and comfort me to such a degree that joy and gladness are coming. I offer You thanksgiving for all You do.

- Psalm 9:1: I will give thanks to the LORD with my whole heart; I will recount all of your wonderful deeds.
- I offer all of my heart to You today in adoring thankfulness. I confess there are dark corners of worry, anger, and frustration that don't want to participate in thankfulness.

Today, as I recount all the amazing things You do, may Your light shine into the darkest place in me, so I overflow with thankfulness to You.

- Thessalonians 5:16–18: Rejoice always, pray without ceasing, give thanks in all circumstances; for this is the will of God in Christ Jesus for you.
- Thank You, Jesus, for everything, even the circumstances that seem impossible to my earthly eyes. Thank You for Your will in our lives. Thank You that every detail is in Your care. Thank You for the power with which You steer our lives to conform to Your will. Help me pray continually today and enable me to rejoice, no matter what.

3

ALWAYS PRAYING WITH JOY

Scripture:

Always offering prayer with joy in my every prayer for you all. (Philippians 1:4, NASB)

Prayer:

Lord, I rejoice in my children. Let every prayer I offer be saturated by joy.

Friday night lights in Texas signify one thing: football. Back in the day when my son donned his pads, I was an avid fan. I rejoiced as I watched him play the game he loved. But watching him stand miserably on the sidelines, edging closer to the coach to see if he would let him play, and then hanging his head as he remained on the bench elicited much different emotions in me. Ones that looked a lot more like sorrow, frustration, and anger.

I would love to tell you I responded with thanksgiving to the Lord for this great opportunity to work in my son's heart. How I offered prayers for my son and his coach with joy. That would be a great story! If it were true, that is.

Unfortunately, what I can tell you is how unproductive stewing and fuming and complaining and sighing are. I can guarantee that not a single one of those activities even resembles joy. When I prayed, "God this is not fair. Please, please, pleassssse let him play," it did not elicit happy feelings. At all.

Paul sets a high standard for our prayers in Philippians 1:4, "***always*** *offering prayer with joy* in my ***every*** prayer for you." (NASB, emphasis added)

Always.

Every.

These are not words that leave much wiggle room for us to justify praying without joy.

Paul uses *always*s in 1 Corinthians 1:4: "I thank my God *always* concerning you" (emphasis added). But when my heart is heavy with concern for my child, whether over something relatively insignificant, like football, or something drastic, like a health crisis, how in the world do I pray with joy?

The only way lies in trusting the Lord and hoping in His ultimate plan. Timothy Keller writes, "Worry is not believing God will get it right, and bitterness is believing God got it wrong."[11] I admit that when I believe God gets it right, I rejoice. But when I don't understand what God is doing or allowing?

No matter the circumstance, God's command to us is: "Rejoice always; pray without ceasing; in everything give thanks; for this is God's will for you in Christ Jesus" (1 Thessalonians 5:16–18, NASB). If I want to line my heart up with the Lord's, I must ALWAYS start with rejoicing.

Before I begin praying, I should rejoice.

While I am praying, I must rejoice.

After I am finished praying, I continue to rejoice.

Not that I praise the difficulty of the circumstance, but I praise the God who holds my child and every problem; the One who can cause all things to work together for good.[12]

God Means It for Good

Sending all his servants from the room, Zaphenath-paneah stood before eleven men. His heart overwhelmed, uncontrollable tears poured down his cheeks.

Because he was in charge in Egypt of the food stored for a famine that had decimated the entire region, anyone needing supplies petitioned Zaphenath-paneah. When the sons of Jacob arrived from Canaan seeking food, they did not recognize their brother dressed in Egyptian finery. But Joseph knew them the moment they stepped in the room.

From the time his brothers first presented themselves in Pharaoh's court in Egypt to buy grain for their families back in Canaan, Zaphenath-paneah had faced his two different identities.

Zaphenath-paneah had been born Joseph, a member of the tribe of Jacob. As a youth, his own brothers had threatened him with murder, but instead decided to sell him to traders who took him to Egypt. Whether his siblings' motivation had been jealousy or rivalry, their intent was to get rid of Joseph, and they succeeded.

As a result, he experienced a thirteen-year roller-coaster, starting as a simple household slave and eventually becoming the trusted manager of affairs in that home. When a false accusation sent him to prison, he languished there until an unlikely reversal of fortunes landed him in his current position, as Pharaoh's most trusted adviser.

At this, their second encounter, the moment had arrived to confront his brothers, the men responsible for his suffering, and to reveal himself. Emotions overwhelmed Joseph. If he desired to vent his anger, he had the power to do just that.

Looking at his brothers, he simply proclaimed, "I am Joseph!" (Genesis 45:3)

Shame and fear struck his brothers. Recognition dawned, as did the realization that their sibling could now exact whatever retribution he desired. But Joseph's response shocked them, as it still convicts all of us who say we trust the Lord.

"So Joseph said to his brothers, 'Come near to me, please.' And they came near. And he said, 'I am your brother, Joseph, whom you sold into Egypt. And now do not be distressed or angry with yourselves because you sold me here, for God sent me before you to preserve life. For the famine has been in the land these two years, and there are yet five years in which there will be neither plowing nor harvest. And *God sent me before you to preserve for you a remnant on earth, and to keep alive for you many survivors. So it was not you who sent me here, but God*'" (Genesis 45:4–8a, emphasis added).

Not only was Joseph restored to his brothers, but eventually he also reunited with his beloved father. But think about this: how could he have enjoyed a joyous reunion with his father if he had given his brothers what they deserved and punished them?

Joseph's faith evaluated even slavery and prison as God's mission. Because God was in charge, he could forgive his brothers and live in joy.

Years later, when his father died, Joseph's brothers began to fear again. Would Joseph take revenge now that their father was gone? Though he again had the power to retaliate, Joseph responded from faith in his heavenly Father.

"But Joseph said to them, 'Do not fear, for am I in the place of God?

As for you, *you meant evil against me, but God meant it for good*, to bring it about that many people should be kept alive, as they are today. So do not fear; I will provide for you and your little ones.' Thus he comforted them and spoke kindly to them."(Genesis 50:19–21, emphasis added)

The Result

Like Joseph, I define our situations and my children's circumstances. Will I wallow in sorrow as I navigate difficulties? Will I blame those who seem responsible? Or will I trust that God is in charge, at work, and up to more than I could ever imagine? Will I believe that He can take even THIS (insert whatever horrible thing weighs down your heart) and cause good to result?

There is only one way I have found to give thanks and respond with joy. Colossians 3:2 commands us to, "*set your mind* on the things above, not on the things that are on earth" (NASB, emphasis added). To SET MY MIND is a definite act of the will. Another translation is to "keep thinking about things above."[13] I must steer my mind continually. If I do not choose to set my mind on what God is doing in His realm, and concentrate on those things, then I am most certainly doomed to be dwelling on all those scary scenarios my worry dreams up.

Thankfulness and joy elevate my thoughts. When my mind is SET on the things above, my prayers are no longer limited to earthly realities or circumstances.

God informs me, "'For my thoughts are not your thoughts, nor are your ways My ways,' declares the Lord. 'For as the heavens are higher than the earth, so are My ways higher than your ways and My thoughts than your thoughts'" (Isaiah 55:8–9, NASB). Joseph used this perspective to move past anger and trust the God whose ways were beyond his earthly understanding.

Unless I set my mind in the heavenlies, I will never think God's thoughts about my child. But once I reorient my mind, I can hope in God's promise, "But as it is written: '*Eye has not seen, nor ear heard, nor have entered into the heart of man the things which God has prepared for those who love Him*'" (1 Corinthians 2:9 NKJV, emphasis added).

When I rest my mind on things above, I can rejoice in the fact that my children are in the hands of He who is able to do far more abundantly beyond all that we ask or think.[14]

The reality is, I can't even conceive all that God is up to in my child's life. But I can offer joyful prayer because I do know He is doing SOMETHING beyond my imagination and for His glory. And that deserves both thanksgiving and joy.

To Be Joyful I Must Be Thankful

So, no matter what I am feeling, I must pray with joy. But if I can't muster up any rejoicing, then I must stop praying.

Wait a minute. Did I just suggest that I STOP praying?

Yes, I did.

I must stop praying long enough to go back to thanksgiving. Returning to Philippians 1:3, "I thank my God in all my remembrance of you," I need to *practice thankfulness* about my child until I can pray with joy. *If I do not feel joy while praying for my children, I am focusing on the present instead of on what God can do.*

When my children were small, we used to play a game called "Thankful." When everyone in the car seemed to be crabby and complaining, I said, "Let's play a few rounds of Thankful." After they groaned for a few seconds, I chose someone to start. There were very few rules to this game. You just had to state one thing for which you were thankful, and you couldn't repeat something someone else had said. Usually the first few rounds were rather boring, as the kids begrudgingly participated by being thankful for the obvious.

After a few rounds, however, all the easy stuff was taken, and they had to get creative. They couldn't just be grateful for lunch or for their parents. What was left to be thankful for? They started to express appreciation for God's plans and His opportunities. As they voiced gratitude at a deeper level, the mood lifted.

Why? Because their perspective changed. They began to peek into the unseen, where God's hand was at work in their lives.

I pray with joy for the same reason my children and I played the "Thankful" game; thankfulness and joy completely change my perspective.

If I skip the step of joyous gratitude, my prayer time dissolves into focusing on what is NOT happening or what I am afraid will happen. I fall into complaining, begging, and suggesting solutions. As if God isn't in control and doesn't know what is going on, I inform Him what my kids are doing wrong, and how He needs to fix them.

But God knows the inner workings of my children's hearts far better than I can ever imagine. He already knows what is happening. He doesn't need me to notify Him.

I just need to begin thanking Him for something. Anything. Thanksgiving has the tendency to snowball, if I will allow it. If I firmly establish a heart of thanksgiving, my perspective changes. The more I praise God, the more I remember. And the more I remember, the more the joy will flow, which is vital because the battle in my mind is between joy and worry. They cannot reside in the same place.

Worry is the emotion of fear. Joy is the emotion of hope.

Worry crowds out joy, and the converse is also true. If *I begin* prayer with thanksgiving, the resulting joy drives out worry.

The battle is constant. As a parent, there are so many emotions and mindsets that rob me of rest: doubt, fear, anger, judgment, condemnation, expectation, and my own selfish plans. Why is it so easy to fall into these traps?

Well, these are my kids I am talking about! I am passionate because I care deeply about their lives—both on earth and for eternity. But I must purposefully channel that passion, or it will morph into the ugliness of a controlling spirit ruled by fear.

Since anxiety prohibits gratitude, I must stop everything and re-adjust. When I find myself stubbornly clutching fear, and ignoring God's available grace, I need to get quiet and start confessing.

I pray:

- Lord, please forgive my prayers of fret and worry.
- Please forgive my doubt in Your power to reach and grab and save.
- Please forgive my reliance on my own judgments instead of Your future plans.
- Please forgive my assumptions that what I see is all there is, and that what I fear is what will happen.

I was not designed to bear the weight of all my concerns. If I try, I will be crushed. But God is the One Who "daily bears our burdens" (Psalm 68:19, NASB). My Jesus walks beside me, daily bearing the burden of my heart of love for my children, wanting me to simply give it to Him, trust in Him, and wait on Him.

I transfer this overwhelming load when I confess my doubts, look to Him to provide solutions, and thank Him for all He has and will do. And then, no matter how dark current situations appear, I am freed up for glorious prayer.

One Last Plank

To trust Jesus and thank Him with joy when situations logically call for anxiety requires not just a transfer of burden but also a change of perspective.

Joy focuses my mind squarely on the One who works in my child, loves my child, and effects change in my child. I can offer prayer in delight because of Christ's work in them, not because of their circumstances. Praying with power and conviction, my hope rests in His plan for my child's future.

So far, from Philippians 1:3–4 we have laid two planks in our prayer platform.

First: we placed the plank of thanksgiving.

Second: we placed the plank of joy.

These two disciplines change my heart and mind and enable me to enter into trust, faith, and hope. The challenge becomes to remain thankful and joyful. That brings us to the third part of our prayer platform: seeing correctly.

What I focus on alters my heart. Like when Joseph looked at his brothers through a view of God's will, I must view my children through the lens of God's hand at work if I want to maintain the right attitude. When I am marked by thanksgiving and joy, and I view my children through the light of the gospel, I will be able to walk in the freedom Jesus designed me for.

PRINCIPLE:

I don't have to feel joy about my circumstance to pray with joy, therefore I should ALWAYS pray with joy.

APPLICATION

Scripture: Always offering prayer with joy in my every prayer for you all. (Philippians 1:4, NASB)

Prayer: Lord, I rejoice in my children. Let every prayer I offer be saturated by joy.

- No matter how you feel right now, offer prayer to the Lord with joy.

Does "always offering prayer with joy" seem impossible to you? If so, why?

List current situations where joy appears impossible. Pray through each one. Release difficulties from your responsibility into the hands of Jesus, so you can pray with joy.

What does the following Scripture mean to you? How can it change your perspective on current worries?

"Eye has not seen, nor ear heard, nor have entered into the heart of man the things which God has prepared for those who love Him."(1 Corinthians 2:9, NKJV)

Play the Thankful game! Write down as many things as you can think of to be thankful for. Go deep. Go wide. Be specific. The Lord is generous, and the harder we look the more we places we will recognize His hand.

Spend a few moments confessing your fears as sin. Then ask Jesus to replace the fear with joy.

Prayers of Joy

The following verses reveal God's desire for us to walk in joy. After each verse is an example of how to pray through the verse. There is also room for you to write your own prayer.

(More Scripture and prayers can be found at **http://www.susankmacias.com/unceasing**)

- Psalm 51:12: Restore to me the joy of your salvation, and uphold me with a willing spirit.
- Lord, I come to You with a burdened heart and confess there is no joy here. Thank You for this verse that promises You can restore what has been lost. I ask You to give me a spirit that is willing to look at our current realities and choose joy. Please fill my heart with Your joy.

- James 1:2: Count it all joy, my brothers, when you meet trials of various kinds.
- This is a tough verse to live, Jesus. But through Your Spirit, I want to respond to my trials with joy. I bring each trial to You, Lord, and, through faith, I count them as joy instead of loss and pain. Please redeem every hardship to Your glory.

- Romans 15:13: May the God of hope fill you with all joy and peace in believing, so that by the power of the Holy Spirit you may abound in hope.
- Please fill me with Your joy, so that my prayers can be fueled by Your hope. Help me to believe and hope in You, however You want to work in my kids. Fill me with so much joy and peace that there is no room for worry.

- 2 Corinthians 7:4: I am acting with great boldness toward you; I have great pride in you; I am filled with comfort. In all our affliction, I am overflowing with joy.
- This is my desire, Jesus—to be so filled with Your comfort that even in my children's afflictions, I overflow with joy.

Help me to boldly proclaim You through the ways I exhibit Your joy.

4

IN VIEW OF THE GOSPEL

Scripture:

In view of your participation in the gospel from the first day until now.

(Philippians 1:5, NASB)

Prayer:

Lord, help me view the ways I participated in the gospel with my kids through the lens of Your truth.

"Everyone okay back there?" Grunts from the recesses of the fifteen-passenger van assured me that the mounds of sleepy teenagers and youngsters were fine.

"We are nearing the border, so everyone needs to wake up and get ready for the crossing." Moans emanated from the sleeping kids. Something about "crossing the border" aroused the most lethargic adolescent male.

With five of our own children, and a few extra teenage boys, our family headed to Mexico on a mission trip to build houses for residents of a border town.

Over one weekend, we built a one-room home. Even without plumbing or electricity, this was a *vast* upgrade to the shack the family lived in at the time.

How wonderful. How godly. How service-minded.

How revealing.

We learned several important lessons that July weekend of ministry. Building a house together, in 105-degree heat, in a place where we should not eat the food or drink the water revealed issues running underneath the surface of our family. It was an educational weekend.

Here are some of the highlights:

- A fourteen-year-old son who chose that weekend to discover exactly how much arguing, talking back, and general disruption he could get away with before his parents cracked.
- Parents who cracked.
- A mom with a three-day migraine headache.
- A surly sixteen-year-old son who snarled and rolled his eyes with regularity while "helping" to build.
- Two little girls unaware they should NOT eat the local food or drink the water. This lesson was thoroughly learned at two o'clock in the morning as they ran to the bathroom. Repeatedly.

Oh, the joys of "participating in the gospel" (Philippians 1:5) together! The joy and thankfulness Paul expresses in Philippians 1:3–4 culminates with this unique phrase in Philippians 1:5. He expresses these positive emotions while viewing their "participation in the gospel," from the first day he met them up to the present moment.

Just like it did for Paul, how we look at the past makes all the difference in how we pray now. This means that even when looking back at our "participation in the gospel together" includes visions of headaches, vomiting, heat, exhaustion, and very bad attitudes, I am still supposed to offer the thanksgiving and joy I observe in Philippians 1:3–4. I admit, it took several years before I learned to see that mission trip to Mexico from the Lord's perspective.

The Greek word for participation used in Philippians 1:5 is "koinonia," which implies something much deeper than being in the same place at the same time. Koinonia means fellowship, and a deep, interdependent relationship that works toward a common goal.[15]

The gospel of Jesus offers us forgiveness we do not deserve and removes our guilt. Instead of punishment, through the cross, we receive forgiveness through the deep, atoning power of His blood. THIS is the gospel in which we fully engage with our children.

My husband and I continue to pursue Christian fellowship with our children. This includes not only taking them to church, which exposes them to the gospel, but also ministering together, where they observe the gospel in action.

Actively participating in Jesus's gospel involves getting our hands dirty together. It could mean going to Mexico and building a home when it is 105 degrees. But it could also mean something less drastic, like making a meal for a family with a new baby; standing together on a street holding pro-life signs and praying; or assisting a ministry that distributes food to the poor or homeless. We might help an elderly member of the church with house projects.

Church and ministry are obvious places where we participate together. But in reality, our family shares in the gospel from the moment we wake up to the moment our heads hit our pillows.

Daily living, although not easy, is very, very real. We repeat the cycle of sinning against each other, confessing to each other, and forgiving each other. I might fake out the people at church about my patience level or my anger management, because in order to do so, I have to hold it together for only a few hours at a time. But my kids? I can't fool them. They have seen the REAL me in all its complicated, contradictory messiness.

Living the gospel is about confronting sin daily. Our family did not need to go to Mexico to practice a gospel mentality. We do it every day.

My children observe me fail and then ask for their forgiveness. They see repentance and forgiveness over and over again. And hopefully, they participate in this glorious cycle that takes them from sinning to conviction to repentance to confession to forgiveness to restoration repeatedly in their own lives.

Family life—it is the gospel in all its 3-D, Technicolor reality.

From the First Day until Now

From the moment a child enters our family, we live and serve and sin and forgive together.

Philippians 1:5 records the time frame of this gospel life, from "the first day until now." It is in the "until"—that space in the middle—where all the messy, beautiful family life happens. What have my kids experienced of the gospel from the first day they were born up to the present? Was it grace, forgiveness, and sacrifice? Was it compromise, hypocrisy, neglect? Or was it legalism, harshness, and restrictions? Honestly, mine experienced a combination of all of those things.

I confess at times I was more worried about my reputation and what the "church people" thought of me than about my relationship with my kids. I've let my own pride in their accomplishments, or embarrassment at their behavior, color how I entered into the gospel with them.

Perhaps your fellowship with your child is broken. Maybe past hurts from an unloving church have soured your child to the church, to the gospel, or even to God.

Within these heartbreaking situations, however, good news still exists. God saved people out of messed-up churches and theologies in the New Testament. He made disciples out of common fishermen and rarefied Pharisees and despicable tax collectors and women of ill-repute. Our children's hearts are not more than Jesus can handle.

The good news is, no matter the state of your children or your relationships, the situation is not hopeless. The current realities may seem impossible, but God wants us to see past our own insufficiencies to His glorious ability.

Oswald Chambers wrote, "... anxiety is apt to arise when we remember our yesterdays.... But God is the God of our yesterdays.... It is true that we have lost opportunities that will never return, but God can transform this destructive anxiety into a constructive thoughtfulness for the future. Let the past rest, but let it rest in the sweet embrace of Christ. *Leave the broken, irreversible past in His hands, and step out into the invincible future with Him*"[16] (emphasis added).

The only way I have found to "leave the broken, irreversible past in His hands, and step out into the invincible future with Him" is to pray. God uses my prayer in His redemptive transformation.

I pray. He works.

Look Toward the Stars

A sigh escaped Abram's lips. Exhaustion, hope, doubt, and relief crowded his mind. *At least Lot and his family are safe again,* Abram thought.

Lot had been captured when Sodom was defeated by an alliance of four enemy kings. As soon as he learned of the incident, Abram led his own men to rescue his relative. When they reached the enemy forces, he attacked at night, defeated them, and recovered Lot.

Eventually, Abram returned home to his own tents. Grateful for the success of the venture but exhausted from the battle, he needed rest and recovery. Instead, he sat awake, wondering about his own family. When would the ultimate fulfillment of God's promise occur?

Abram's voice echoed in his empty tent, "Maybe I misunderstood what He meant when He promised a great nation would come from me. When we left Haran and came here to Canaan, Sarai and I were old already. We barely hoped for a child anymore. Now, ten years later, it is even more hopeless than when the promise first came. Could I have misunderstood?"

Suddenly, Abram became aware of the mystery of the presence of God, and the Lord's word filled his mind: "Fear not, Abram, I am your shield; your reward shall be very great."[17]

Maybe from the weariness of battle, maybe from the doubt of the delay of the fulfillment, or possibly from a heart so confident in its relationship, Abram dared to question the Lord. Whatever the motivation, Abram ventured to point out the problem: "Behold, you have given me no offspring, and a member of my household will be my heir."[18]

The God of heaven and earth could have become angry at Abe's doubt. He could have condemned his impatience. But, instead, the Lord lovingly took the time and gave Abram a new set of glasses.

"And He took him outside and said, 'Now *look toward the heavens*, and count the stars, if you are able to count them.... So shall your descendants be'"[19] (emphasis added).

As he gazed at the sky resplendent with innumerable stars, I wonder if Abe's heart filled with thanksgiving and joy. Back in Haran, when God promised to make him a great nation, could Abram have dreamt that meant a number past counting?

From that moment on, all Abram had to do was look toward the heavens to see what God had planned. He would need that visual reminder, for it would be another thirteen years before God changed his name to Abraham and finally granted him and Sarah a son, whom they named Isaac.

Even then his waiting days were not over. Isaac waited forty years to get married. Then he and his wife Rebekah were barren for twenty more years before the birth of Esau and Jacob. God made Abram wait seventy-three years from vision to grandchild, the hope of generations that would continue.

How could Abraham hope through so many years of promise without fulfillment? He learned to look at the barrenness in view of the promise and power of God. He didn't look at his one grandchild to see God's plan. He looked at the stars.

Likewise, with our own children, we pray not in view of their problems or our failures. Instead, we look toward the Lord, and pray in view of the gospel—the redemptive power of Jesus. This is the Jesus who "is able to do immeasurably more than all we ask or imagine, according to his power that is at work within us" (Ephesians 3:20, NIV).

This Is Prayer

With this corrected vision, I pray in view of the promises of the Lord. This has transformed not only what I pray but also what I understand prayer to be in the first place.

Prayer is my mind and heart agreeing with God that what He says is true, what He does is good, and what He will do is right.

Prayer is speaking God's truth into the impossible.

Prayer is shining God's light into the dark recesses where nothing else can reach.

Prayer is seeing the current reality through the corrective lenses of hope and confidence in His ultimate outcome.

Paul said his thankfulness and joy were in view of the Philippians' participation in the gospel. As I pray for my kids, I require Jesus to correct my view of the past so I can also do that.

Honestly, I have too many regrets to view our past and maintain the right attitude on my own. There were incidents when our kids were hurt by experiences in the church. My husband and I did not always make the right decisions. That makes it hard to work past the guilt or anger to get to the joy.

I must ask the Lord to help me see as He does. Only then can I pray while looking back with thanksgiving and joy for it all. Even the messy bits.

Am I saying you can look back on even THAT (whatever "that" is) with thanksgiving and joy?

Yes, yes, a thousand times yes! If you and I want to pray powerfully for our children's present and future, then we MUST trust God with their past. Even the parts we messed up!

Think again about Abraham. This is a man who really messed up. Twice, he traveled into Egypt and tried to pass off his wife Sarah as his sister. He slept with his servant Hagar to have a son, just in case God needed a little help making this great nation thing happen. He was not a perfect man. But God worked in him and used him anyway.

The Lord uses me and my kids anyway, too. I must learn to look at every situation the Lord allowed in our lives and proclaim thanksgiving and joy over it. I only accomplish that if I believe He can and will redeem it all in their lives.

I recognize there are very destructive situations that can occur with our kids, and I believe these grieve God. Sin always does. But there is nothing outside of the redemptive hand of our gracious and compassionate Father. He can and will transform it, when we allow Him.

Parenting is hard. There is just no way around that fact. Hebrews 10:32 states, "But remember the former days, when, after being enlightened, you endured a great conflict of sufferings" (NASB).

Enduring a great conflict of sufferings is a perfect definition of parenthood. As Christian moms and dads who work, pray, and war for our children, we are not just striving for them to have good manners and get through school. We also desire they know truth and follow Jesus, which makes us primed for a conflict of sufferings on steroids.

The writer of Hebrews continues, "Therefore, do not throw away your confidence, which has a great reward. For you have need of endurance, so that when you have done the will of God, you may receive what was promised" (Hebrews 10:35–36, NASB).

Okay, so mistakes have been made in the past. We have suffered. Everything that has occurred in my family has not been pretty. But hope is not lost, God is not done, and His promises still stand.

"But we are not of those who shrink back to destruction, but of those who have faith to the preserving of the soul" (Hebrews 10:39, NASB). Hear that? No. Shrinking. Back.

So, here is the game plan:

- I will not throw away my confidence, no matter what the circumstances look like.
- I will have endurance.
- I will do the will of God—and it is always His will that I pray.
- I will not shrink back.
- I will pray for my children with thanksgiving and joy, remembering all that we have gone through together in the

past and pressing forward into all that God will do in the future.
- I will look toward the heavens and put my glasses on.

Put on Those Glasses

Remember the two planks of our prayer platform we already laid: thankfulness and joy. Those two steps get our minds and hearts lined up with the Lord in our prayers.

This last plank, *correcting our vision*, is just as important. Without the right glasses, I will not see clearly. Paul prays for the Ephesians, "... that the eyes of your heart may be enlightened, so that you will know what is the hope of His calling..." (Ephesians 1:18a, NASB). The eyes of my heart experience enlightening when I see as God sees.

I agree with Scripture and confidently proclaim, "God sees not as man sees, for man looks at the outward appearance, but the Lord looks at the heart" (1 Samuel 16:7, NASB). I know I do not see as God sees. I would never look at five loaves of bread and two fish and think it was enough food to feed a crowd. I would never see a ninety-year-old, infertile couple and think they were the perfect candidates from which to start my chosen people.

I know, in practical reality, the detriment of not seeing well. I need visual correction every day to function. If I don't have my glasses on, I can't even make a cup of coffee. Correcting my vision with the proper spectacles changes everything. I am transformed into someone who can get things done. Putting on my glasses is like a daily, miniature miracle.

Prayer is spiritual spectacles. If I don't look back on our past through the lens of trust, then I will dive into the wrong end of the pool, hitting my head in the shallowness of worry. With corrected vision, I plunge headfirst into joy, changing my perspective to confidence in God's plan.

Once joy and thankfulness are in place, I am prepared to view my children's participation in the gospel from the first day until now through God's eyeglasses and trust Him completely for my children's past, present, and future.

So Prayer Mama: lay aside guilt, regret, pride, worry, anger, or any other attitude that blurs God's future plans. Leave the past in God's hands.

Be thankful. Feel joyful. Put on your spectacles and see faith in action.

From this platform you are ready to launch into confident, powerful, God-honoring, life-changing prayer.

PRINCIPLE:

If I view our past through faith in the Lord, I can pray for our future with confidence.

APPLICATION

Scripture: In view of your participation in the gospel from the first day until now. (Philippians 1:5, NASB)

Prayer: Lord, help me view the ways I participated in the gospel with my kids through the lens of Your truth.

- Put on God's glasses as you begin your prayers. Ask Him to help you see as He sees.

Koinonia means fellowship, and a deep, interdependent relationship that works toward a common goal. In what ways does this describe your family's experience together in church or Christian ministry?

According to Philippians 1:3–5, our thanksgiving and joy come, at least partly, in the view of how we have participated in the gospel together.

What memories bring you joy?

What memories bring you sorrow, anger, or frustration?

Oswald Chambers wrote that we need to "leave the broken, irreversible past in His hands, and step out into the invincible future with Him." List below those areas you need to leave with Jesus. Be honest about your regrets. Then spend time in prayer giving them into the Redeemer's hands.

Now comes the hardest part! Ready?

Look back at the lists in the last two questions and thank God for every one of them. He can build a mighty testimony of His power to restore and redeem, no matter what happened. The enemy wants you to wallow in the poison of grief and anger that never ends. Jesus wants you to trust Him with your worst pain and to thank Him for what He will do with it.

Prayers for Corrected Vision

Jesus healed blindness in many people. He even created sight in a man born blind from birth. He is able to do the same with us. The following verses reveal different ways we can pray for the Lord to correct our vision so that we can walk in thankfulness and joy.

(More Scripture and prayers can be found at **http://www.susankmacias.com/unceasing**)

- Matthew 20:32–34 (emphasis added): And stopping, Jesus called them and said, "What do you want me to do for you?" They said to him, "Lord, let our eyes be opened." And *Jesus in pity touched their eyes, and immediately they recovered their sight and followed him.*
- Jesus, I, too, need You to touch my eyes and restore my sight. I become blinded by problems and challenges. I only see how I can't fix things instead of seeing Your steadfast power. Please have pity on me and open the eyes of my heart.

- Ephesians 1:17–18 (emphasis added): That the God of our Lord Jesus Christ, the Father of glory, may give you the Spirit of wisdom and of revelation in the knowledge of him, *having the eyes of your hearts enlightened*, that you may *know what is the hope to which he has called you*, what are the riches of his glorious inheritance in the saints.

- Please give me Your Spirit of wisdom and revelation so I can know You and walk in the hope You give. The eyes of my heart need enlightenment in order to see the magnitude of what You do. Please give me the faith to leave the future with You and to live in joy and thankfulness now.

- Isaiah 35:4–5 (emphasis added): Say *to those who have an anxious heart*, "Be strong; fear not! Behold, your God will come with vengeance, with the recompense of God. He will come and save you." Then *the eyes of the blind shall be opened*, and the ears of the deaf unstopped.
- Lord, I give my anxious heart to You. Thank You that You are a God who comes and saves. Please open my eyes to see as You see. And please open my child's eyes to see You clearly. Thank You, Lord.

- Acts 26:18 (emphasis added): *To open their eyes, so that they may turn from darkness to light* and from the power of Satan to God, that they may receive forgiveness of sins and a place among those who are sanctified by faith in me.

- Open my eyes, Lord! Open them that I might see Your light and rest in it. Thank You for the forgiveness You bring that never runs out. May I be a shining ray of Your light as I walk in joy and thankfulness.

PART III

THE POSITION

THE POSITION OF PRAYER

And I am sure of this, that He who began a good work in you will bring it to completion at the day of Jesus Christ. It is right for me to feel this way about you all, because I hold you in my heart, for you are all partakers with me of grace, both in my imprisonment and in the defense and confirmation of the gospel. For God is my witness, how I yearn for you all with the affection of Christ Jesus.

— Philippians 1:6–8

The first step to effective prayer required me to build my prayer platform. That accomplished, I moved from worry, guilt, and frustration to thankfulness, joy, and vision. Learning to trust the Lord carries amazing benefits!

But this book is not about making me happy, it is about powerful prayer for my kids. Yes, I want to move out of stress and worry. But I do not spend hours praying for my children so I will feel better. If that was all it was about, I could just stop at the step of thankfulness and joy.

I desire the deeper things of God for my kids, so I labor unceasingly in prayer to fuel that movement. A diving platform, unless used to perform a beautiful dive, is just a flat surface, ridiculously high up. Likewise, a prayer platform will not be effective unless I use it to dive into prayer.

The summer I conquered my fear of the high dive, my friends and I became experts at "the pencil." That is the fancy name we gave for jumping straight off the high board. We embellished it with a straight, stiff body, pointed toes, and arms stretched taut above our heads. Impressive, don't you think?

Not surprisingly, the sense of accomplishment eventually wore off, and I was ready to attempt harder moves: the front dive, the back dive, even a flip. Those were precarious days. When performing a flip it was VERY important to rotate 360 degrees. Too little, and I landed on my back. But too much, and I face-planted into the water. I sometimes belly flopped so hard it almost knocked the wind out of me.

I began to study neighborhood divers who performed dives with rhythm and precision. They used the same position every time. The more I mimicked their positions, the more successful I became, resulting in a less painful summer.

In the end, the position of my body determined both the beauty, and the pain level, of my dives.

Diving required discipline and control. I couldn't think about the height of my platform or fear the potential pain from a mistake. Instead, I focused on my actions and my dives improved.

Posture and position affect my prayer life, as well.

Philippians 1:6–8 gives two key principles to maintain the right position in my prayers:

1. Confidence in God's love and work in the lives of my children.
2. Loving my kids like Jesus does.

Instead of focusing on my kids' problems, I use my "corrected vision" (verse 5) to look to Jesus. From that perspective, I rest my confidence in God actively working, whether I can currently observe it or not. This may sound easy. Sure it is. Just as easy as an inward three-and-a-half flip in pike position with a few twists thrown in for good measure.

Maintaining my position of confidence in God's continual work, as well as healthy relationships with my children, is one of the hardest tasks I face. But it is vitally important. I love them so much, I can lose balance. I strive to help them be successful. I want to keep them from harm or pain. But a fine line exists between help and manipulation.

I easily belly flop in my attempts to help my kids. If I try to help my kids without looking first to Christ, I cause pain, like belly-flopping, knock-the-breath-out-of-you, pain.

The temptation to assist the Lord, in case He is busy, trips many a parent. Good intentions get in the way just as easily as bad ones.

God will have His way with my children; my mistakes will not stop that. I am not saying I can impede God's plan. But I do think sticking my grubby hands into the works can slow things down. And I know it can adversely affect my relationships.

Since my nagging voice can be a distraction from His still small whispers to them, I have learned to ask myself a series of questions.

- Am I an impediment to God's work in their lives? Or am I a catalyst?
- Do I drown out His still, quiet voice? Or do I amplify it?

- Am I a road block to God's plans for them? Or am I an entrance ramp?

A healthy prayer position keeps me in an appropriate posture. Deep prayer forces me to take a step back and examine my attitudes and actions. It maintains my confidence in God and preserves a loving, grace-infused affection toward my children.

On the diving platform that summer long ago, I maintained my position. Legs straight. Toes pointed. Precision, accuracy, and strength. Those were the necessary steps.

In prayer, I also practice position. Before God. Knees bent. Heart submitted. Confident that God is in charge. Loving my children with the affection of Christ. This position radically alters WHAT I pray.

Are you ready? It is time to start our dive into the deep, clear waters of God's will.

5

CONFIDENT OF THIS

Scripture:

And I am confident of this very thing, that He who began a good work in you will perfect it until the day of Jesus Christ.

(Philippians 1:6, NASB)

Prayer:

Lord, thank You for being at work in my child. I am confident of all You are doing.

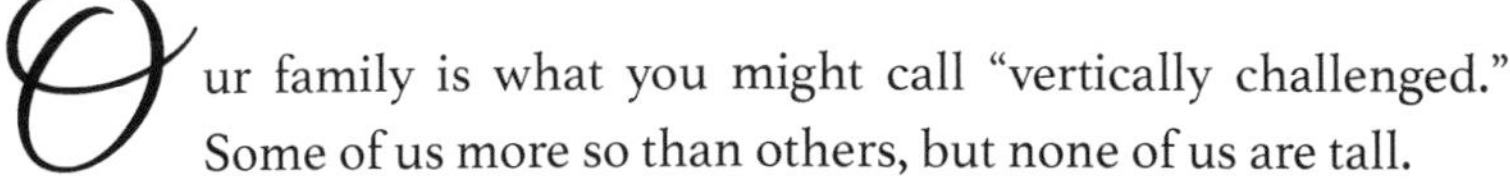

Our family is what you might call "vertically challenged." Some of us more so than others, but none of us are tall.

When my second son, the shortest, suited up in pads and football uniform to take the field, he did not appear a menacing force to the opposing team. They probably perceived him as the least of their worries.

But no one told *him* that.

He knew he was shorter than everyone else. He just didn't care. He understood the game of football. He loved it and played it well. I stood on the sidelines for two years, cheering like a crazy lady, wide-eyed with amazement as my son led his team in defensive tackles, ran like a man on a mission, and played his heart out. What he lacked in size, he more than made up for with passion and ability to outmaneuver his opponents.

He was confident. And that made all the difference.

There Are Giants in the Land

He reminds me of Caleb and Joshua in the book of Numbers.

While fleeing slavery in Egypt, the Israelites watched God perform amazing miracles. God forced Pharaoh's hand with ten successive plagues that nearly destroyed Egypt. After opening the Red Sea to create a safe passage, He gave the Israelites His law. He provided manna every day so they didn't starve as they trekked through the desert.

Finally, leading them by a pillar of cloud and fire, He guided them to the land He had promised them. Camping on the border of this Promised Land, the people were on the edge of the fulfillment of their hopes. They were almost home.

At the command of the Lord, Moses sent one man from each of the twelve tribes on a spying expedition. The spies investigated the land and its inhabitants. After forty days, they returned. Having observed fertility and abundance, they brought back samples of the large fruit that grew there.

But they also brought reports of big, strong, dangerous inhabitants who possessed the land. What could a bunch of freed slaves do against giants?

"They are too strong for us!" ten of the spies proclaimed, infecting the camp with growing fear. The people cried out. Had they come so far for nothing? Were they now doomed to die in the desert? It would have been better to remain in slavery.

But the other two spies, Caleb and Joshua, didn't view the giants from the perspective of their own strength. They compared the giants to God. And God trumped the giants at every turn.

Listen to the words of Caleb and Joshua to the people: "The land which we passed through to spy out is an exceedingly good land. If the Lord is pleased with us, then He will bring us into this land and give it to us—a land which flows with milk and honey. Only do not rebel against the Lord; and do not fear the people of the land, for they will be our prey. Their protection has been removed from them, and the Lord is with us; do not fear them" (Numbers 14:7b–9, NASB).

Unfortunately, the people grabbed rocks and threatened to stone Caleb and Joshua. *Fear and anxiety do that. They silence bravery and confidence. They see the problem and not the One with the solution. Fear and anxiety walk in avoidance rather than victory.*

What does this story have to do with prayer, particularly prayer for our children? Well, everything, actually.

If your kids are anything like mine, they have several "giants" in their lives. Destructive giants like addiction, rebellion, or rejection. Lumbering giants like laziness, apathy, or lack of faith. Or perhaps pernicious ones like anger, pride, or selfishness. Fear. Abuse. Peer pressure. There are too many to name.

As a parent, even a praying parent, I quickly become overwhelmed and fearful as I look into the eyes of these giants UNLESS I keep my eyes on the Lord.

I have no confidence in my own or my children's ability to face our problems. But my confidence in God's ability to not only face but conquer those giants is immeasurable.

Look where Paul places his confidence in Philippians 1:6, "For I am confident of this very thing, that He who began a good work in you will perfect it until the day of Christ Jesus" (Philippians 1:6, NASB).

While Paul was joyful and thankful for the church at Philippi, his confidence rested in God, not them! Paul's certainty lay in the work God had begun in their lives and His ability to continue that work until Jesus came back.

Paul did not trust his own abilities, either. Paul could exhort these believers through his letter, but He could not fix them. That was God's job.

There are two vital points that apply directly to how I pray.

1. God, not me, began His work in my child.
2. It is His responsibility to complete it, not mine.

These two facts are key to obtaining freedom from the burden and weight of my child's spiritual life. Those burdens result from taking responsibility God never gave parents. If I want relief from anxiety and shame, then I must agree with this verse.

God is in charge of the time schedule, not me! Because God *begins* and *completes* the work, I must let Him determine how and when He will finish it.

You may be asking yourself, "Then what am I supposed to do? Just sit around and twiddle my thumbs while my child makes bad choices or wastes time?"

No!

You are supposed to pray! Unceasingly and wholeheartedly!

That is what you are supposed to do.

A Tale of Two Moms

I must stay diligent to keep my confidence in God and not myself. It grieves me when I realize I have more self-confidence than God-confidence.

Below is a tale of two moms to illustrate the difference between mom-confidence and God-confidence. Since you are my friend, I will warn you. Potential toe-stepping-on may occur.

Meet Christy.

Christy and her husband tried to raise their three children "right." They went to church, emphasized academics, trained character, and most of all, loved their children dearly. The first two kids attended college, preparing for careers.

But Jake, the baby of the family, resisted college in favor of concentrating full time on his band, the band that had practiced in Christy's garage for the last two years. The one she eagerly anticipated never practicing in her garage again.

One night, Jake sat down with his parents and said, "Mom and Dad, I don't want to go to college. I want to give my band a real chance. Playing music is my passion. It is all I want to do!"

The ensuing disagreement included escalating emotions and volume. Christy tried to act as mediator between father and son, even though she agreed with her husband. After a night spent behind slammed doors, where restless sleep was clouded by bad dreams, Christy now stared into her coffee. She formulated the perfect little speech to help Jake see the foolishness of his plan. Hearing him descend the stairs, she straightened herself up and drew breath to speak. But as he entered the breakfast room, Jake cut her short. He raised his hand and beat her to the punch.

"No, Mom. Don't. Don't start. I know you want what is best for me, and that you love me. But you've have spent the last two years telling me your plans. They were always about my giving up my band and going to college.

"You've dropped hints and told me stories about bands that fail. You've nagged me about college applications, put school brochures in my room, and told me how useful a business degree is. I just need you to stop nagging me!"

"Nag? *Nag*? I do *not* nag, Jake."

"Alright, Mom. Alright. But I really don't want to talk about this anymore." Jake threw his words over his shoulder as he made a hasty retreat out the front door.

Jake's accusations resounded through Christy's head the rest of the day. As she went about her day, she repeatedly assured herself, "I am not a nag!" She only did what all mothers do. She helped.

While folding clothes she recalled how she asked him about every assignment, reminded him of due dates, and daily asked how classes were going. Of course, she forced him to complete applications and coerced him on college visits. She just wanted the best for him. After all, what mom doesn't make sure her man-child gets enough sleep, eats well, dresses decently for church, and participates in the "best" extracurricular activities?

The term "hover-mother" floated through her mind as she drove to the store. "I do not hover. And I am not a nag," Christy assured herself. "I am a mother, and I am just doing my job!"

"In fact, I am the one who let him go to music camp!" she realized. She began praying out loud, "Oh, God, is that where this started? Is it my fault? Did I push too hard or not push hard enough?"

Collapsing into an armchair, she buried her face in her hands, "Oh, Lord, please help me."

Now meet Janice.

She walked down the street that morning as Jake bolted from his house, but barely noticed him. Her mind was far away. With a heavy heart, she talked with her Lord. Once again Janice brought her second child, Audrey, before the throne. Audrey had always been THAT child. Adventurous, stubborn, and determined to create a better world, Audrey lived life at full throttle. She played as hard as she fought for what was right.

“Father, thank You for this stubborn child who cares so much about her ideals. Please help her to always line her convictions up with Yours. Let her be stubborn for You and Your will.”

Audrey not only had decided to teach in an impoverished, inner-city elementary school but she also felt called to live there.

Audrey had explained to her mom, “I can’t just pop in and out of their lives. I have to be in the community to really affect them!”

Sighing, Janice prayed, “Alright, Lord. You gave me this idealistic, stubborn girl. What do I do? I am worried about her safety and for the realities that she cannot understand. She has no idea what she is getting herself into, does she, Lord? But You do. You know exactly what is happening, and I ask You to guide each one of her steps.

“And I beg you, Jesus—please give me wisdom. I need to know what to say and what *not* to say. When do I offer advice and when do I keep my mouth shut?”

Continuing her walk, Janice remembered years ago when Audrey was in tears over chemistry. Janice had fought her desire to fix it. Instead, she sat with Audrey’s tear-stained cheek on her shoulder and reminded her of James 1:5, “But if any of you lacks wisdom, let him ask of God, who gives to all generously and without reproach, and it will be given to him” (NASB).

Then she had taken Audrey’s hand and they asked God to open Audrey’s mind and give her understanding. Funds were tight and they couldn't afford a tutor. But they had asked God to send help. Within a week, a neighbor offered assistance and they made her dinner in exchange. Between the neighbor, hard work, and continuous prayer, Audrey passed chemistry. But the most enduring lesson came from Audrey experiencing God answering prayers in real ways.

"Thank you, Jesus, for living in Audrey. I ask Your Holy Spirit to give her wisdom, faith, and clear direction. This scares me to death, but as long as she is in Your will, You will keep her. I place my confidence in You. You started this, and You will need to complete it.

"Would you comfort this mama's heart and help me trust You more?" A sly grin spread over her face as she concluded, "And, by the way, Jesus, thanks for putting her in such a scary place. As long as she lives in the inner city, You and I will get to spend LOTS of time together."

Her spirit settled and her heart at peace for the first time that morning, Janice picked up her pace and asked the Lord who else she could pray for as she continued her walk. Suddenly, her neighbor, Christy, came to mind. "You want me to pray for Christy, Lord? Sure, but she seems to have everything together. I wonder why You want me to pray for her."

Which One Am I?

If I am going to react like Janice instead of Christy, I am going to have to fight my own inclinations. Which of these would I rather be? A nagging hover-mother with a God complex and martyr syndrome? Or a hopeful, faithful mom who seeks wisdom by trusting in the Spirit?

Well, when you put it that way...

I told you toes might get stepped on.

When I try to take on God's job in my child's life, my actions harm my relationship with my kids. Not only that, the news gets worse. That "God complex" behavior accomplishes nothing! Absolutely nothing.

Oh, the irony. I want to affect real change in my kid's eternal lives. I worry, cry, and beg God to act. When He doesn't move quickly enough, I nag and manipulate. But I can't drag my kids into God's will, no matter how hard I try.

I must choose between trust in my work and my children's efforts and trust in God's work in their lives. Hoping in God transforms my attitude. Since God begins and completes His work in their lives, I cannot take the credit for anything. I also cannot take the blame for every wrong choice they make.

It is easier to walk in confidence of God's hand directing my kids' lives when I know exactly what He has promised. His meaty, trustworthy promises can be used as a direct prayer request.

Just look at this list of what the Father promises:

- He died for them while they were yet sinners. -Romans 5:8
- He convicts them of sin. -John 16:8
- He causes them to be born again to living hope. -1 Peter 1:3
- He makes them alive in Christ even when they are dead in trespasses. -Ephesians 2:4–5
- He reveals to them a wrong attitude. -Philippians 3:15
- He never leaves or forsakes them. -Deuteronomy 31:6
- He cares for them and their troubles. -1 Peter 5:7
- He is with them and strengthens, helps, and upholds them. -Isaiah 41:10
- He is a refuge, strength, and help for them during trouble. -Psalm 46:1

- He has plans for their future. -Jeremiah 29:11
- He restores their soul and leads them in paths of righteousness. -Psalm 23:3
- He guards them against the evil one. -2 Thessalonians 3:3
- He fills them with joy and peace. -Romans 15:13
- He keeps His covenant and steadfast love to a thousand generations. -Deuteronomy 7:9

Why would I ever get in the way of all God does? Instead, I want to get on God's bandwagon for my child. From there I can bombard heaven, thanking God for His promises, asking for their fulfillment, and believing them. God will do exactly what He says He will do.

"God is not man, that he should lie, or a son of man, that he should change his mind. Has he said, and will he not do it? Or has he spoken, and will he not fulfill it?" (Numbers 23:19)

It might not look like my dreams. It might not happen on my time schedule. It might have different results than I imagine. But it will occur because, "For as many as are the promises of God, *in Him they are yes*" (2 Corinthians 1:20a, NASB, emphasis added).

> Don't be discouraged—the grace you've been given is inexhaustible and unstoppable. It will finish its work.[20]
>
> — Paul David Tripp

But, as it is written, "What no eye has seen, nor ear heard, nor the heart of man imagined, what God has prepared for those who love him."

— 1 Corinthians 2:9

PRINCIPLE:

When my confidence is not in myself and not in my child, ***but in Jesus,*** *I can keep praying and trust God to work.*

APPLICATION

Scripture: And I am confident of this very thing, that He who began a good work in you will perfect it until the day of Jesus Christ. (Philippians 1:6, NASB)

Prayer: Lord, thank You for being at work in my child. I am confident of all You are doing.

- Where is your confidence? Take a moment and ask the Lord to help you trust Him more.

In the Old Testament story, Caleb and Joshua trusted God more than they feared the giants in the Promised Land.

Think about your kids. Are there any giants they struggle with? List them below.

Spend time asking God to defeat those giants. You might want to write the list down and post it somewhere that will remind you to pray for their defeat.

Philippians 1:6 contains two principles:

- 1. God begins the work in my child
- 2. It is His responsibility to complete it

What about this verse gives you comfort and hope? How will this affect your prayers?

As you read the story of Janice and Christy in this chapter, which mom did you identify with more?

If you feel convicted of "hover-mother" attitudes, this is a good time to stop, confess, and allow Jesus's forgiveness and healing to begin transforming your heart.

How can you release your child to God's care?

Prayers for Confidence in God's Work

It is easier to remain confident in God's work in our kids when we realize what that looks like.

(More Scripture and prayers can be found at **http://www.susankmacias.com/unceasing**)

- Deuteronomy 7:9: Know therefore that the LORD your God is God, the faithful God who keeps covenant and steadfast love with those who love him and keep his commandments, to a thousand generations,
- I praise You, Father, for Your constant and faithful love. Thank You for Your constant and unending work in our lives. May we, and the generations that follow, never cease serving You.

- 1 Peter 1:3: Blessed be the God and Father of our Lord Jesus Christ! According to his great mercy, he has caused us to be born again to a living hope through the resurrection of Jesus Christ from the dead.

- Praise You, Jesus, that You cause us to be born again. Please take my child and cover him/her with Your great mercy. I rest in Your work in his/her heart, and I ask You, in Your time, to cause him/her to be born again.

- Romans 15:13: May the God of hope fill you with all joy and peace in believing, so that by the power of the Holy Spirit you may abound in hope.
- I give my child to You and ask You to fill him/her with Your joy and peace and cause his/her heart to believe in You fully. I hope in You, not in my child. May the power of Your Holy Spirit cause our whole family to abound in hope.

- Isaiah 41:10: Fear not, for I am with you; be not dismayed, for I am your God; I will strengthen you, I will help you, I will uphold you with my righteous right hand.
- Oh, Lord, I confess I am fearful of the road my child is on. I find myself dejected and hopeless every time I take my eyes

off of You. I ask You, Lord, to fulfill the promises of this verse. Please give me strength, help me, and sustain me with Your hand. I ask the same for my child. Please give him/her strength, help, and support. I ask You to help me trust in Your work in his/her life.

6

WITH THE LOVE OF JESUS

Scripture:

For it is only right for me to feel this way about you all, because I have you in my heart, since both in my imprisonment and in the defense and confirmation of the gospel, you all are partakers of grace with me. For God is my witness, how I long for you all with the affection of Christ Jesus.

(Philippians 1:7–8, NASB)

Prayer:

Lord, I ask You to help my heart love my children with the love of Jesus.

Waking up to the gentle sound of raindrops, I roll over, nestle down, and sigh. Absent is the energy to get out of bed. Missing is the resolve to face another day. Pervasive weariness weighs down my heart. There are simply too many big hurts for me to get dressed. In fact, never getting out of bed again seems a viable alternative.

A formidable list of needs hounds me. Just ten months ago, we celebrated our first son's wedding. But last week his wife walked out. His devastation resounds in my soul, and grief chokes my heart. My husband's start-up business is failing, as are our finances. His despair feels like lead in my gut. My second son is giving up his dream job to help his older brother. My third son flounders in high school, my younger daughter's dyslexic mind refuses to cooperate with phonics, and my other daughters are lost in the vacuum-like middle. Why get out of bed and face all that?

What am I feeling? Despair. Sorrow. Anger. Fatigue. Confusion. I am a fixer, but I cannot fix anything. I cannot alleviate the pain or mend the problems. I cannot adjust the sails to extract us from this storm. I have no idea what to do.

Fast-forward to the present. Even six years after our family endured this crucible, my heart constricts and unbidden tears spring to my eyes. How did we ever survive that valley of the shadow of death? There is only one answer: Jesus.

This concentrated devastation trained me in the unsurpassed value of prayer. I experienced its value all the way down to my toes. I didn't pray because I felt like it. I prayed out of the desperate realization that there was nothing else I could do. Then I discovered there was nothing better I could do.

Paul understood tough circumstances. He endured two years of imprisonment in Caesarea, followed by a long sea voyage that resulted in shipwreck and a venomous snake bite. Paul wrote his letter to the Philippian church from Rome, where he resided under house arrest. Up to this point in his ministry, Paul had experienced beatings, stoning, fleeing in the middle of the night, imprisonment, abandonment, and more. If Paul let his circumstances or feelings dictate his response, we would read a very different letter to the Philippian church.

Like Paul, I must not allow circumstances to dictate my reactions, or allow harsh situations to strangle my prayer life. What seemingly impossible obstacle exists in your child's life? What problem shakes your confidence in God's ability to work this out to completion? What fear lurks in your mind so much that you dare not say it out loud, much less pray about it?

Here is the secret: we must speak our darkest fears aloud in prayer to our Lord. If we are ever going to get in the position of effective prayer, we have to tackle our emotions and bring them to the cross, even if we have to hog-tie and drag them there! Then we can pray, and pray, and pray.

But I Don't Feel Like It!

Our current culture sets great stock in feelings. Our emotional response is portrayed as a reflex over which there is no control, just like a knee responding to a doctor's rubber mallet applied to the reflex.

I choose to challenge that thinking in myself. While my initial reaction may flow from my gut, my actual response needs to originate from somewhere further north. How I act needs to come from my mind.

Paul states in verse 7, "For it is only right for me to feel this way about you all." As a mom, I admit I often justify frustration, anger, or despair as the right way to feel. Those, however, do not lead to a victorious prayer life. Really. They don't. You can trust me on that one.

I don't usually associate feelings with my mind, but the word "feel" in this verse is translated "think" in other versions. The Greek word is *phroneō* and is translated "set your mind" in Matthew 6:13, Mark 8:33, and Romans 8:5.[21] I like the words "set my mind." I picture myself picking my feelings up by the scruff of the neck and setting them down exactly where they need to be—in God's care. Only then do I have the opportunity to align my feelings with God's truth.

My thoughts and emotions are intricately interwoven, and they are stubborn. They cling to offense and obsess about the worst possible outcome. Only continuous effort keeps them in line.

In our family's darkest days, daily, hourly, and even moment by moment decisions were required to set our minds back on God's truth. Nothing was clear, and our outcomes were uncertain. But returning to the Word, we found the Lord had not moved. He was still in charge and still held us during the storm. No matter how wretched I felt, He did not change.

The Affection of Jesus

I often struggle to remain in the right position so I don't belly flop in my prayers. Philippians 1:7 starts with, "...it is only right for me to feel this way about you all...." The deep and complex feelings common to motherhood make maintaining the right position difficult.

Paul tells the Philippians, "I have you in my heart." My children reside in the very roots and fibers of my heart. When they succeed, I rejoice. When they hurt, I suffer. When they fail, I grieve. Consequently, as I try to pray, these complicated, interwoven emotions tie me up in knots.

But here is some good news. Paul felt precisely the same way. While maybe this is not exactly "good" news, at least we know we are in good company! Paul wrote to the Colossians, "For I want you to know what a great conflict I have for you" (Colossians 2:1, NKJV). If Paul was "in conflict" over his own disciples, then I understand better my own conflict over my kids.

Paul continued his hope for the Colossian church, "that their hearts may be encouraged, being knit together in love" (Colossians 2:2, NKJV). And there you have it, the perfect definition of parents and children: "knit together." But, let's be honest. There are a LOT more emotions in this knitting process than just love. The intricate and often messy pattern includes some feelings that try to separate us more than interweave us. This very complexity mucks up our parental prayer lives.

The solution?

It is right there in Philippians 1:8b, "the affection of Christ Jesus." What a freeing affection that is. The love of Jesus strips away personal plans and expectations. It gives rather than takes. It covers rather than blames. It forgives rather than remembers. It showers equally on worthy and unworthy.

THAT, my friends, is the affection required for me to be in the right position to pray effectively.

Do I want to pray with power? Yes. I absolutely do.

Then I HAVE to lay aside grief, anger, frustration, fear, anguish, and concern. These emotions might be justified and realistic. But holding onto them muddies my prayers and burdens my heart. To successfully rid myself of the burden, I must lay them at the right place—at the foot of the cross. Jesus can handle them much better than I.

Thinking back to my family's crucible time, there were days when my prayers were moanings too deep for words. Jesus met me there and held me. The Holy Spirit interpreted those cries as prayers to the Father.[22] But eventually I needed to move out of that stage. Like Paul, who prayed while chained in prison, I had to pray while broken in spirit. I didn't feel like it, but I did it anyway.

This does not just apply to the emotion of despair. Whether frustrated at bad choices, angry at habitual disrespect, worried over continued problems, or hopeless about issues with no apparent solution, we must leave them with Jesus to move into God's throne room with our prayers.

A small miracle often occurs as we move in obedience contrary to our feelings—God begins to transform our feelings and line them up with His truth, sometimes inch by tiny inch. The more I prayed when I didn't feel like it, the more I found I felt like praying. I even desired to get up and get dressed and make dinner. I began to see the needs of others and get my focus off my grief. My affections changed from just the emotions of "Mom" to the affections of Christ.

God slowly transformed my insides to want Him more than anything. And THAT - that changed everything. It was no longer about what I wanted. It was about what the Lord wanted. That blew my prayers for my hurting children up into the stratosphere. That launched my prayers for my husband to the moon. That lifted my heart, that heavy, aching heart, to the heavenlies.

We All Need Grace

In Philippians 1:7, grace is the final ingredient for correct positioning in my prayers. I need grace, and my children need grace. They are "partakers of grace with me" (Philippians 1:7b, NASB).

If you have been in church long, you have probably heard much about grace, yet it seems a difficult concept to pin down. A popular definition is, "God's unmerited favor." I prefer the way theologian J. I. Packer defined it: "In the New Testament grace means *God's love in action towards men who merited the opposite of love*. Grace means God moving heaven and earth to save sinners who could not lift a finger to save themselves"[23] (emphasis added).

Daily I partake long and deep of God's active love toward me, when I KNOW I have earned the opposite. Oh, praise the Lord, who gives me the opposite of what I deserve! I can't save myself. I can't pay for my sins. I can't muster the strength to conquer all my bad habits or alter every bad attitude.

Getting a handle on my own desperate, continual need for grace allows me to not be alarmed at my kids' same need. It makes no sense to be surprised at their sinful hearts. Do I perceive their bad choices as a personal affront on how I raised them? Or does the fact that they should know better (since I am the one who taught them!) breed frustration?

As I see my profound need for grace reflected in my children, I should identify with them. We share the requirement for drawing from the same deep well. God's gift covers my darkest sin, every past mistake, and each foolishness of my life. It is also sufficient for my children.

Like beautiful perfume, grace permeates every space. It covers negative emotions that cripple my prayers. It corrects my vision so that I can see my children as equal partakers of grace with me. It transforms my prayers so they can give off that same beautiful aroma.

My prayers are transformed as I ask God to call my child to drink from this life-giving well. Released from the bondage of the need to control and fix my kids, I am opened to God's desires for them and in position to pray with confidence and power. Any fixing to be done will have to be accomplished by the divine Fixer, and I can rest in the confidence that He will complete the job.

From the platform of thankfulness, joy, and corrected vision, I can begin to dive into prayer. I discipline my heart, mind, and body into a position of confidence in His work in my child. My feelings about my child are secured to the cross, and my trust rests in Jesus's love and grace to cover us both. With all that, I can now dive deep into powerful petitions for my children.

> The right way to pray is to stretch out our hands and ask of One who we know has the heart of a Father.[24]
>
> — Dietrich Bonhoeffer

PRINCIPLE:

When I set my mind and heart on truth, and when I love my children with the love of Jesus, I will confidently pray for our heavenly Father's grace to cover all our needs.

APPLICATION

Scripture: For it is only right for me to feel this way about you all, because I have you in my heart, since both in my imprisonment and in the defense and confirmation of the gospel, you all are partakers of grace with me. For God is my witness, how I long for you all with the affection of Christ Jesus. (Philippians 1:7–8, NASB)

Prayer: Lord, I ask You to help my heart love my children with the love of Jesus.

- Honestly take stock of all the emotions you are currently experiencing toward your child. None of what you are feeling is a shock to the Lord. Let Him heal you and fill you with His love.

What experience have you endured with your family that makes it difficult to pray? Is there a place of such deep pain that you are having trouble moving out of it?

Giving Jesus your unmet expectations, hurt feelings, disappointments, and anger frees you to pray with power. Take some time and honestly list burdens you are carrying.

Do you want freedom from the weight of the list above? It is time to give them to Jesus! Spend some time praying through each item. "Set your mind" on the throne of Jesus, set your children at the foot of the cross, and let His grace wash your mind and soul.

Paul told the Philippians they were "partakers of grace with me." Likewise, our children require God's grace with the same intensity we do. As you meditate on that thought, write down areas of your kids' lives that are in need of grace right now.

Ask the Lord to deal with each item you wrote down above.

Prayers for Loving Like Jesus

(More Scripture and prayers can be found at **http://www.susankmacias.com/unceasing**)

- Jeremiah 32:39: I will give them one heart and one way, that they may fear me forever, for their own good and the good of their children after them.
- Thank You for the promises in this verse. Please give each member of our family:
- One heart that follows Your one way.
- A holy fear of You.
- A desire to follow You for ourselves, our children, and our children's children.

- 1 Peter 3:8: Finally, all of you, have unity of mind, sympathy, brotherly love, a tender heart, and a humble mind.
- Lord, I ask You to give a unity of heart and mind between my children and myself. I ask You to give my spouse and me tender hearts and humble minds that we would treat our children with sympathy and brotherly love.

- John 15:10, 13 (NASB): If you keep My commandments, you will abide in My love; just as I have kept My Father's commandments and abide in His love...Greater love has no one than this, that one lay down his life for his friends.
- Lord, please keep my feet, my heart, and my mind so

planted in Your love that I would desire only obedience. My life is Yours to do with as You wish. Like You laid Your life down for me, please help me lay my life down for my kids that they may know You and Your love.

- John 13:35 (NASB): "By this all men will know that you are My disciples, if you have love for one another."
- Please enable me to give a love I don't always feel, that You would be known in our home. Please lead me so that my kids know I am Your disciple by how I love them.

- 1 Peter 4:8 (NASB): Above all, keep fervent in your love for one another, because love covers a multitude of sins.
- I ask for Your love to flood our family. Overwhelm us with it. Even when my children are walking away from You, show me how to love them in way that You are seen. Thank You for covering my many sins with Your love.

PART IV

THE PETITION

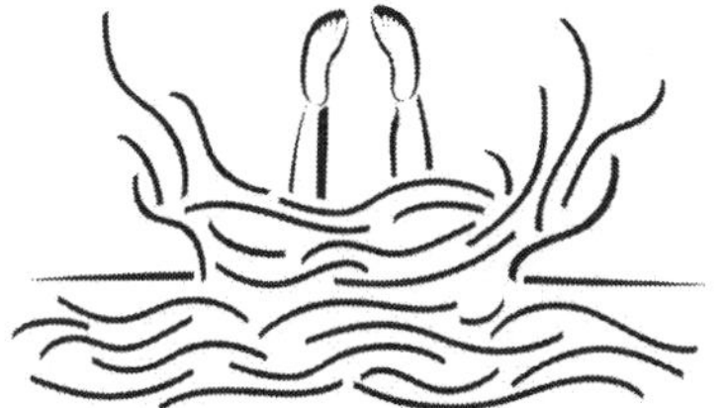

THE PETITION OF PRAYER

And this I pray, that your love may abound still more and more in real knowledge and all discernment, so that you may approve the things that are excellent, in order to be sincere and blameless until the day of Christ; having been filled with the fruit of righteousness which comes through Jesus Christ, to the glory and praise of God.

— PHILIPPIANS 1:9–11, NASB

After diligently building the prayer platform and positioning ourselves in confidence and servant-hearted love, smothered in grace, we are ready to pray. Now—finally—we are getting to that heaven-storming prayer we have been alluding to all along!

It may not surprise you that conquering my childhood fear of the high board, perfecting the swan dive, and learning a front flip at my local swim club never propelled me into the Olympics. My diving career was uneventful and short-lived, though for a few short months in the summer of 1973, I entertained some lovely dreams.

David Boudia is another story, however. At the 2012 London Olympics, David barely advanced through the preliminaries. After a strong semifinal round, he advanced to the finals, where he found himself tied for second with a Chinese diver. In the face of unbelievable pressure, David walked out on the thirty-three-foot platform, executed flawless position and form, and performed the dive of his life. He won the gold.

How did David Boudia perform so well under pressure? Those of us who could never muster enough courage to walk out to end of that platform, much less jump off, focus on his innate talent and ability. But honestly, even David admits it took him years to conquer his fear and be truly comfortable at the platform height. His fearlessness and impeccable positioning flowed from hours of hard work, practice, and effort. As a result, on that day in 2012, he put it all together and won the gold.[25]

All it took was relentless practice over years and years of David's life!

How do we become accomplished at praying? The same way: relentless practice over years and years of our children's lives. What? You thought this would be easy?

To accomplish Olympic-level praying, we pray from the right platform, in an effective position, over and over again.

Please realize that this book is not about finding the correct way to pray. I often start praying the moment something pops up. 1 Thessalonians 5:17 (NASB) states, "pray without ceasing," which means even our thoughts can be a continual conversation with God.

A great variety of prayers are found in the Bible. Prayer can involve moaning, begging, and complaining. My parenting career has included many "Oh, God!" "Help," and "Please, dear God, no!" prayers. Those can be right and good for the moment.

However, I faltered when I wallowed in despair. My spirit, locked to my worst fears, became anchored to grief. I needed desperately for God to lead me out of my self-constructed prison. Through the use of these verses in Philippians, He did just that. He brought me out of worry through thankfulness, joy, and a corrected vision. He released me from the burden of anxiety and fretfulness through confidence in His work and His grace. Then I started praying His desires rather than my own.

Oh, the freedom. Oh, the joy!

To stand on the towering platform in agreement with God's work in my kids freed me from my self-imposed prison. My prayers soared as well, not because I performed well or earned God's hearing. Rather, I was riding the current of God's will instead of trying to drag Him into my plan.

My desires for my kids are often temporal and earthy. God wants so much more for them. I want education, jobs, and happiness. God wants wisdom, excellence, and fruit. I crave temporal success. God plans eternal effectiveness.

But guess what? When I throw off anxiety and replace it with joy, when I repeatedly thank God for all He has already done, and when I rest my confidence in His vision for their lives, my petitions for my kids change.

If you are wondering what those petitions should be, don't worry. God never leaves us guessing. Philippians 1:9–11 is a guide where He tells us exactly what to pray for, and that is what we will look at next.

Are you ready for heaven-knocking, hell-shattering prayer? Let's go!

> ***Don't worry about anything; instead, pray about everything. Tell God what you need, and thank him for all he has done.***
>
> — PHILIPPIANS 4:6, NLT

7

ABOUNDING LOVE

Scripture:

And it is my prayer that your love may abound more and more, with knowledge and all discernment.

(Philippians 1:9)

Prayer:

Lord, please cause my child's love for You and Your will to overflow.

Love lies in the eye of the beholder.

"She is so cute, I think I am in love."

"I love pizza."

"I don't love soccer as much as football. In football, you get to hit people."

"I love travel and adventure."

"I have to get this dress! I just love it!"

"All the Marvel® movies are fantastic, but I *love* Captain America!"

My kids tend to casually throw the word *love* around. However, when Paul prayed that the Philippians' "love may abound more and more," I can state with utmost confidence that he was NOT hoping their love for pizza would overflow.

With the word *love* deployed with little specificity, the definition becomes fuzzy. But I have a powerful mental picture of love by which to measure its true meaning.

Some childhood memories hang on long after the details fade. The parts that remain are what impact a life. From my childhood hearkens a memory of love fleshed out.

I was twelve when my grandfather, whom we called Pop, was diagnosed with late-term lung cancer. Knowing he was very sick, we traveled as often as possible to visit him in the last six months of his life. But strangely, my recollections of that time are not as much of him as of my grandmother.

We called her Mom, because when we were born she just didn't feel old enough yet for a grandmother name. Quiet, reserved, and elegant, she always seemed in control, at least through the eyes of a child. She was kind, though not necessarily warm. Yet, in those final months of my Pop's life, I watched her care for him in ways that left an indelible mark in my mind. I observed her bathing, feeding, quietly encouraging, and caring for him to the end. I remember few words she said. But my memory of her actions and demeanor scream "LOVE!"

As an adult, now old enough to be privy to secrets adults keep from children, I have learned that on parallel tracks with her love must have traveled a great deal of fear. Pop did all the business of the home. She had no knowledge of budget, bills, or their financial status. She stared into a scary future. Her life companion, the man who took complete care of her, was dying. Yet, as far as I saw, she didn't waste her last few months with him worrying about what was coming. And because she didn't, the fragrance of love pervades my memories from those painful times.

"Love bears all things, believes all things, hopes all things, endures all things. Love never ends" (1 Corinthians 13:7, 8a).

Love is an action. It places another's interest above itself. It serves and sacrifices. It soothes and ministers. It comforts and calms. It lays itself down over and over and over again.

Jesus purely and perfectly lived THIS love as He humbled Himself to become a man so that He could make atonement for our sins. "By this we know love, that he laid down his life for us, and we ought to lay down our lives for the brothers" (1 John 3:16). Oh, how He loves us, and because He does, we experience a perfect example of what true love looks like.

THIS love, I pray, invades my children's hearts. I beg God this love will control their actions, guide their decisions, and direct their work.

Paul didn't pray for the Philippians to just possess this love, he prayed they would abound with it. But what does abounding love look like?

What Is Abounding Love?

For our thirtieth wedding anniversary, my husband and I decided to travel somewhere we always wanted to visit. As we grow older, we realize the bucket list items only get checked off by actually doing some of them. Niagara Falls was a long-time resident on my list, with the added benefit of being next door to Buffalo, the original home of Buffalo Wings. We could grab wings on our way to the Falls. Considering our stomachs is always essential when planning vacations.

After stopping in Buffalo for lunch, which lived up to our expectations, we headed to Niagara. Standing at the edge of those Falls and watching the massive amounts of water descend, we were speechless. The magnificence drove the memory of those delicious wings from our minds. Later we donned attractive blue ponchos and rode a boat right to the bottom of the Falls. Staggering amounts of water crashed around us. It was abounding.

Abounding is not a word in our common vernacular any more. When Paul prayed the Philippians' love would abound more and more, we need to grasp what he was actually asking. Abounding love looks much more like Niagara Falls than a quiet stream. It is extravagant love.

At the risk of mixing my metaphors, I offer another word picture, albeit a sort of weird one. For some reason, the word "abounding" makes me think of jumping around, I suppose from the word "bounding" being such a prominent part. When I think jumping, I picture Tigger. Yes, Tigger, Winnie the Pooh's irrepressible friend. Tigger never realizes how extraordinarily over-the-top his actions are, though you do have to give Rabbit kudos for trying to give him insight. I believe most human interactions can be explained after a thorough reading of Winnie the Pooh. Case in point, the explanation of our current word. Tigger perfectly illustrates what "abounding" love looks like: exuberant, effusive, fill-up-the-room-wherever-it-appears. He is the stuffed animal version of Niagara Falls.

The Greek word translated abounding is "*perisseuo.*" Even if you don't care a whit about the Greek, you will "love" the connotations of this word, which means: overflowing, excess, to be so richly furnished as to have abundance, to have so much that there is more to spare.[26] No matter how you look at it, that is a whole lot of love!

When we are praying for our kids to have abundant love, we are praying that they would have such excess love that it would overflow out of their lives into the people and places surrounding them. I find it impossible to pray this for my kids without praying it for myself at the same time. Abounding love resembles Tigger because it is impossible to ignore. It invades the room, transforms the mood, and changes every dynamic around it.

First, the bad news. On our very best day, our deepest love will not come close to a Tigger-bounding, Niagara-crashing type of love. It is just too earthly and selfish.

Here is the good news, whether for ourselves or for our kids: God never expects us to create this kind of love in ourselves. I John 4:7a states, "Beloved, let us love one another, for love is from God...." Love is *from God*! We do not have to feel this love or will it into existence. It is not from ourselves. Nor can our kids conjure up godly love on their own. This extraordinary love comes from the Father.

Just a Little Bread and a Few Fish

At the end of a long day in the Galilean countryside, a large crowd grew increasingly hungry. Listening to Jesus all day filled their souls with wonder, but now their stomachs demanded some attention too. Jesus assigned His disciples the job of feeding the five thousand people.

Has Jesus ever asked you to do something impossible? I can just imagine the disciples looking at each other in disbelief. Was He serious? Even if there was bread to buy (which there wasn't), they possessed no money to purchase it. Their idea had been to send everyone home to take care of themselves (Matthew 14:15), but, instead, Jesus asked them to meet the crowd's needs. Philip tried to inject some practicality into the conversation by informing Jesus, "Two hundred denarii worth of bread is not sufficient for them, for everyone to receive a little" (John 6:7, NASB). Thanks, Philip. I am sure Jesus had no idea it would cost so much, or He would never have asked.

Andrew attempted obedience. He apparently went through the crowd asking if anyone had any food on them, because he informed Jesus, "There is a lad here who has five barley loaves and two fish, but what are these for so many people?" (John 6:9, NASB). Andrew may not have had enough faith to believe Jesus could work with such a paltry amount, but at least he tried.

I love that John tells us the bearer of the loaves and fish was a lad. Neither Matthew nor Mark include this detail in their accounts. But, as parents, we should not gloss over this fact. A youth held the ingredients for the miracle. Jesus is not limited by our kids' age, ability, or possessions. Instead, He takes meager offerings, from people others would ignore, and causes them to abound.

You are probably familiar with the rest of the story. Jesus had the disciples tell the people to sit down in groups. "Jesus then took the loaves, and when he had given thanks," (John 6:11) ... HOLD THE PRESSES! Did you see that? Do you mean *the very first thing* that Jesus did was to give thanks? For what? Five loaves and two fish?

Just like the very first plank on our prayer platform, when Paul writes in Philippians 1:3 (NASB), "I thank my God in all my remembrance of you," Jesus begins His prayer with giving thanks.

Our Savior modeled many of the principles in Philippians 1:3–11. He began with gratefulness, but He wasn't thanking God for the insufficiency; He thanked God for what was there. And in view of what the Father had done in the past, He anticipated with confidence what would happen next. He was preparing to share the abundance of the gospel with everyone on that hillside.

After Jesus thanked the Father for the bread, He distributed it to those seated, repeating the action with the fish. When the crowd's hunger was satisfied, Jesus instructed the disciples to gather the fragments that were left, "that nothing may be lost" (John 6:12). I think He wanted to teach them, and us, a very important principle.

From those five loaves and two fish, the disciples filled twelve baskets with leftovers. Now brace yourself, because the word for leftovers in John 6:13 is the exact same Greek word that is translated "abounding" in Philippians 1:9! Jesus's ability to make our kids' love abound is not limited by how much there is to start with, any more than His ability to feed the crowd was limited by the quantity of food with which He began.

Think of this on a personal level. The love I have to give on a daily basis for my marriage, my kids, my home, my work, or my anything else is usually insufficient. There are just more needs than my love can cover, like needing-enough-for-five-thousand-and-only-having-enough-for-one-lunch type of insufficient. But God can take my meager offerings and multiply them to abounding proportions.

Paul promised the Philippians, "...my God will supply all your needs according to His riches in glory in Christ Jesus" (Philippians 4:19, NASB). He based this on his own experience with the Lord, from whom he had "received everything in full and ... [had] an abundance..." (Philippians 4:18a, NASB). Want to guess what word is translated abundance in Philippians 4:18? It is the same Greek word for abounding. Paul has so much there are leftovers!

Now apply this to our kids. I want my children to serve Jesus with their whole heart. I desire that they love what Jesus loves and follow Him wherever He leads. But what if I see quite the opposite? I could nag or use guilt to plague them into church. Or I might worry at night instead of sleep.

Well, if you have read anything up to now, you already know those reactions, though tempting, are off limits. No worrying. That is the rule. Another rule is to start with thanksgiving. Like Jesus, take the little bit you have and thank the Father for what He is going to do. And then start praying that your child's love will abound so much it overflows his or her heart and becomes uncontainable.

Just picture your child's heart with such an abundance of love for the Lord that there are leftovers!

THAT- that is what we are praying for.

And may the Lord make you increase and abound in love for one another and for all, as we do for you.

— 1 Thessalonians 3:12

We love because he first loved us.

— 1 John 4:19

PRINCIPLE:

The Lord's ability to cause my child's love to abound and overflow is dependent only on His power, so I can ask for that with confidence.

APPLICATION

Scripture: And it is my prayer that your love may abound more and more, with knowledge and all discernment. (Philippians 1:9)

Prayer: Lord, please cause my child's love for You and Your will to overflow.

- Ask the Lord to multiply your child's love for Himself and for the things the He loves.

What does your child love?

What do you hope he/she will grow to love?

Do you have a memory of an example of love lived out? If nothing comes to mind, write about an example from something you have read or heard about.

Paul prays the Philippians' love will abound. When you hear the word *abound*, what do you think of?

Now describe "abounding love." What would that look like to you? What would it look like in your kids?

When Jesus fed the five thousand, he started with a small amount and ended with twelve baskets of leftovers! Since the Greek word for leftovers is the same as that used for abounding in our Philippians Scripture, does this change your idea of what you are praying for when you pray your kids' love will abound? In what way?

Prayers for Abounding Love

God's standard for love, set by Jesus, is high. "The Lord is merciful and gracious, slow to anger and abounding in steadfast love" (Psalm 103:8).

We cannot muster this kind of love on our own, nor can our children. It is not natural. Instead, it is supernatural. That is why we must pray for the Lord to build this in our kids.

(More Scripture and prayers can be found at **http://www.susankmacias.com/unceasing**)

- Luke 6:38: Give, and it will be given to you. Good measure, pressed down, shaken together, running over, will be put into your lap. For with the measure you use it will be measured back to you.
- Lord, I ask You to fill my child with so much love that it would be beyond measure. May his/her love for You and Your plans spill out onto everyone with whom he/she comes in contact. As he/she gives that love away, I ask You to refill his/her tank over and over again.

- 2 Thessalonians 3:5 (NASB): May the Lord direct your hearts into the love of God and into the steadfastness of Christ.
- Please direct my child's heart away from the plans of the world and toward You and Your love. Please allow the steadfastness of Jesus to steer his/her heart continually toward You.

- Romans 5:5: And hope does not disappoint, because the love of God has been poured out within our hearts through the Holy Spirit who was given to us.

- Thank You so much for promising to pour Your love in our hearts. I ask You to pour, through the power of the Spirit, Your love into my child's heart. Please bring hope by the presence of Your love in our hearts. We cannot truly love without You.

- Jude 1:2, 21–22: May mercy, peace, and love be multiplied to you ... keep yourselves in the love of God, waiting for the mercy of our Lord Jesus Christ that leads to eternal life. And have mercy on those who doubt.
- Please multiply Your mercy, peace, and love so that we recognize there is more love available than we could ever imagine. I give my child to You today and ask You to rain that multiplied love down on him/her. Have mercy on the areas of doubt in his/her life and fill those empty places with Your love. Please help him/her stay in Your love and help him/her be patient, waiting on You. As an adult, I confess I have a hard time with delay. How much more difficult it is for my child, with the impatience of youth. Yet, You are worth it. I ask You to surround my child with such an extravagance of Your love that he/she will be willing to wait on You.

8

REAL KNOWLEDGE AND DISCERNMENT

Scripture:

And this I pray, that your love may abound still more and more in real knowledge and all discernment.

(Philippians 1:9, NASB)

Prayer:

Lord, please grant my child the knowledge and discernment needed to live for You in this world.

I have never been the smartest girl in the room. In high school, I was friends with the smart kids, but I didn't attend the advanced classes with them. I studied hard and liked to read, which helped me succeed in school, but I was always aware that there were "smart kids" and there were "normal kids." I belonged to the latter category.

Never have I perceived my lack of knowledge more than when I had kids. Motherhood smacked any previous self-confidence right out of me. I am pretty sure the same thing occurred when the smart kids became parents. Knowledge of quadratic equations provides little instruction on dealing with colic or on successfully navigating sleep deprivation. Children have a way of leveling the playing field.

My first stage of motherhood required a huge knowledge leap for me. My own mother, an excellent homemaker, ran a shipshape house. I grew up securely in a family with one sister and a well-behaved father. We kept bodily noises to ourselves and observed manners at every meal. It always smelled good in our house. God must have been chuckling as I assumed all families looked and smelled like ours.

My husband grew up in a very clean home, but a male-dominated one. His mom and sister had little hope of exerting a feminine influence on the four males in their house. The first dinner I ate there, I sat in amazement at the absence of my normal. There was no gentle passing of each dish, taking a reasonable helping, and leaving plenty for others. Instead, it all happened at once and it was each man for himself. If you wanted food, get it on your plate. The fact that my mother-in-law is a fabulous cook just increased the voracity.

But my real culture shock arrived as I gave birth to three sons in three and a half years. Never before had I experienced that much testosterone. My boys shocked me with things they said, smells they made, and antics they tried. The fact they were so close in age and shared a room amplified the effect. I was out of my league and needed wisdom, knowledge, and discernment every moment. And lots of air freshener!

My sister also had three boys in rapid succession. That's right, my parents, who raised two quiet, doll-toting, dress-upping, book-reading girls, were the grandparents of six grandsons. They created a playroom for the boy-cousin gang with toys from our childhood. If it was possible for the toy to break, a boy broke it the first day. I guess we all had culture shock and needed a new understanding.

Eventually girls were added to the mix and the hormones averaged out a bit. But before that, I found myself desperately seeking help. In school, when I struggled with a class, I knuckled down and studied hard. So that is how I tackled this problem. I read every book I could find. I sought advice from mothers of other boys. I tried to emulate families I admired.

In the end, I discovered that copying other families was like trying to wear someone else's clothes. They didn't quite fit and were always a bit uncomfortable. I learned tidbits of wisdom from my quest. But if we were going to raise *these* boys in *this* family, we needed a custom fit. The only reliable place to find that was the Source of wisdom. My husband, my boys, and I all shared the same heavenly Father, who created this family. We needed to go to Him to figure out *our* best identity.

Anybody Lacking Wisdom?

Almost every day I am aware of situations for which I do not possess sufficient wisdom. When this happens, I now know exactly what to do. During my personal quiet time, many years ago, God shone a light on a particular verse for me. Seriously, there may have been angels singing and clouds rolling back. That is how profoundly this Scripture leapt out to me.

James 1:5 (NASB) states, "But if any of you lacks wisdom, let him ask of God, who gives to all generously and without reproach, and it will be given him." Here are my takeaways:

- There will be times I lack wisdom.
- God is ready when that happens.
- He does not blame me for not having wisdom.
- I need to ask God for wisdom.
- God promises to generously give the wisdom I need!

Whew! That is a lot of promises for one verse.

I testify, through much experience, that this verse is true. Every time I cried out, asking God for wisdom I desperately needed, He provided. I can't say the clouds rolled back or the angels sang, but an answer always showed up.

Just like me, my kids require knowledge and discernment. As a parent, I am ready and willing to be their fount of wisdom. But there is a problem. From the moment the two-year-old proclaims, "I do it myself!" a line in the sand is drawn by the obstinacy inherited from Adam.

My children are no different than my husband and I. Human pride rarely allows us to admit our needs and problems. Likewise, our kids seldom desire advice, much less instruction. Of course, as parents, our job is to train them anyway, but this tendency does explain much of the tension between parents and children.

Wouldn't it be lovely to sit our teenagers down on the sofa, explain every lesson we learned in the school of hard knocks, watch them absorb our wisdom, and then have them walk out the door and never repeat our mistakes? Yes, *that* would be lovely.

But there is only one place they can obtain real knowledge and discernment. When Paul saw the Philippians in need of these precious commodities, he asked God to grant them.

Praying for knowledge and discernment in our own children has never been more vital. As I look at our culture, I fear for the world in which they will live. But I have no control over their future, just like moms in every previous generation. All I can do is pray for their state of mind and heart within whatever circumstances they find themselves.

Some Guys in Need of Wisdom

Several thousand years ago, there were multitudes of heartbroken, worried moms in Jerusalem. After years of ungodly rulers and war, the land of Judah lay defeated, and King Nebuchadnezzar took the young men who were the cream of the crop back to Babylon. Among them trudged Daniel, Hananiah, Mishael, and Azariah, the latter three becoming famous with their Babylonian names of Shadrach, Meshach, and Abednego. These four were part of a large group who were relocated to the king's household.

Can you imagine watching your precious child being led away to a foreign, pagan land? You could never again see their face, speak into their life, or hug their neck. What would you do? What would I do? I think I would simply collapse and try to will myself to never breathe again. But eventually I would have to scrape myself off the floor, face another day, and pray. Oh, how I would pray that my child would remember the Word of God and not leave Him. And I would cling to the promises that God would never leave or forsake my child.

How did these young men survive to be heroes of the faith in Babylon? While I like to imagine their faithful, Jewish mamas covering them in prayer from Jerusalem, that is not something Scripture tells us. But the book of Daniel does inform us, "God granted Daniel favor and compassion," and "God gave them knowledge and intelligence in every branch of literature and wisdom" (Daniel 1:9, 17, NASB). The knowledge and wisdom the young men needed to thrive in a pagan culture were GIVEN. They were gifts.

Daniel, Hananiah, Mishael, and Azariah decided to believe God, honor His commands, and live for Him in idolatrous Babylon. No matter what names they were bestowed, their hearts were God's. God gave them the knowledge they needed. And were they ever going to need it!

One day, early in his residence in Babylon, Daniel answered a knock at the door to find the captain of the king's bodyguard ready to kill all four of them. In fact, the captain had the task of slaying all the wise men in Babylon. Why? What had happened for such a harsh decree?

It turns out, King Nebuchadnezzar had awakened from a deeply disturbing dream and called the wise men of the court together to tell him its meaning. But the catch was that he wasn't telling them the dream. They would have to tell him what he dreamed, then interpret it. The learned men of Babylon, dumbfounded and terrified, said, "There is not a man on earth who can meet the king's demand, for no great and powerful king has asked such a thing of any magician or enchanter or Chaldean" (Daniel 2:10).

King Nebuchadnezzar would take no excuses. Because they could not do what he demanded, he passed a death sentence on all of his wise men.

I don't know why Daniel and his friends were not in the throne room that day. Maybe they were too young, or still being trained. Possibly they were excluded because they were foreigners. Whatever the reason, they still shared the fate of the others who failed the king's command. Daniel appealed to the king and begged for time to declare to him the dream and interpretation, which was granted.

Daniel went home to his friends and let them know what they were up against. I can feel the stress and pressure in the room as they faced a problem that was unsolvable in their own strength and abilities. They needed a strategy to accomplish the impossible task that the wisest men in the nation could not. Instead of worrying or brainstorming, they held a prayer meeting and asked God to reveal the mystery. They prayed, and their lives literally depended on the answer.

And God answered. What was impossible to man was easy for God.

Daniel's prayer of thanksgiving to God for the answer and vision He gave them shows us, as parents, great insight into what God is able and willing to do. Here are a few excerpts from Daniel 2:20–23:

- "Wisdom and power belong to Him." (v. 20)

- "He gives wisdom to wise men and knowledge to men of understanding." (v. 21)
- "It is He who reveals the profound and hidden things." (v. 22)
- "You have given me wisdom and power." (v. 23)
- "You have made known to me what we requested." (v. 23)

We pray to this same God when we need wisdom. The God we beg to grant discernment to our kids, is the Lord who owns all the wisdom and power, and for whom NOTHING is impossible. He is the God who gave revelation to four scared youths in a pagan land, and He gives revelation to us in our current need.

This same God answered Paul's prayer that the Philippians' love would "abound more and more in real knowledge and discernment" (Philippians 1:9b).

That Is Great for Them, But...

What excuses are you rolling around in your mind, right now, about why this won't work with your child? These excuses usually begin with, "Yes, but..."

I bet I have used some of those same excuses in my own mind, like: my son doesn't even want God's wisdom, my daughter rejects God's truth, my child hates church, she thinks the Bible is a book of myths, and on and on.

These statements may be true at the present time, but *our children's obstinacy or difficulties do not limit the might of God*. Praying in faith requires me to shut down the excuses and press into truth instead. I pray boldly because of who my Father is, and what He can do. Praying for real knowledge and discernment in my kids, in spite of how they may currently be living, places faith in our Lord's power in the face of impossibility.

Since we know from Proverbs 9:10, "The fear of the Lord is the beginning of wisdom, and the knowledge of the Holy One is insight," I pray that my kids fear the Lord. To fear Him means they recognize God is in charge and they will love, respect, and obey Him. For those that don't yet know the Lord, this is a prayer for salvation. For those who walked away from their childhood faith, this is a prayer for a renewal or rebirth of this biblical fear. But even my kids who walk with Jesus need to have their "fear" refreshed periodically. I need to unceasingly continue this prayer, every day I have breath.

Paul tells the Colossians "...we have not ceased to pray for you, asking that you may be filled with the knowledge of his will in all spiritual wisdom and understanding" (Colossians 1:9). No matter their current spiritual status, I do not cease this prayer for my kids. God can pour so much spiritual wisdom and understanding into their hearts and minds that it washes out any deception the world has implanted.

Does it presently feel impossible for your child to receive God's wisdom? Maybe it seems even more unlikely he or she will believe and obey it. Is it as impossible as knowing a foreign, pagan, despotic king's dream and then interpreting its meaning, which included centuries of coming kingdoms? Because that seems pretty impossible. But it wasn't, not when Daniel prayed to our all-knowing Lord and waited for and believed His answer.

I Need That Kind of Wisdom

When my boys were little I needed wisdom to navigate their constant compulsion to wrestle, compete, argue, destroy, rebuild, and conquer. Then, when my girls came along, I needed a brand-new batch of wisdom to recalibrate to feminine attributes, which registered in different proportions in four girls of decidedly unique personalities. Often my prior knowledge, based on being a girl myself, didn't even help.

I may not have served an unreasonable king with unreasonable demands, but being a mother of seven made me aware daily of my desperate need of divine intervention.

Based on Daniel's prayer and James 5:1, here is my prayer as a mother:

Dear Lord, since all wisdom and power belongs to You, would You give some to me today? I do not know what to do next, or exactly what each child needs, but You do. Thank You for willingly and generously giving wisdom when I ask for it. Thank You for loving my child and wanting the best for him/her. Please show me what to do next.

I don't have to be the smartest kid in the room to parent my children. But I can be a discerning parent for my child when I allow myself to be a vessel for God's wisdom.

In the same light, I can and must pray for real knowledge and discernment in my kids' lives. Because, just like four young men in Babylon, boy, do they need it!

> I have been driven many times upon my knees by the overwhelming conviction that I had nowhere else to go. My own wisdom and that of all about me seemed insufficient for that day.
>
> — Abraham Lincoln

PRINCIPLE:

Since the Lord invites me to ask for wisdom, I can pray for wisdom, discernment, and knowledge for myself and for my child.

APPLICATION

Scripture: And this I pray, that your love may abound still more and more in real knowledge and all discernment. (Philippians 1:9, NASB)

Prayer: Lord, please grant my child the knowledge and discernment needed to live for You in this world.

- Think of a specific place where your child needs some wisdom. Take a minute and ask the Lord for that right now.

Are there any areas of parenting where you recognize how much you need God's wisdom? List them and be as specific as possible.

Think about the promise God makes in James 1:5, "But if any of you lacks wisdom, let him ask of God, who gives to all generously and without reproach, and it will be given him."

Now look at your list above. Spend some time asking the Lord to give you the wisdom He promises to give generously.

Do the same exercise with your children. What are areas you can see where they need God's wisdom? List them, and again, be as specific as possible.

You might want to copy this list on a separate piece of paper and put it somewhere you will see it often and remember to pray.

God granted wisdom to Daniel and his friends to survive life in Babylon. When you see the world in which your kids live, for what do you think they will need wisdom in order to walk confidently with the Lord all their days?

We all have our "yes, but..." excuses in our heads about our kids. What challenge seems so large in your child's life that it feels as if it is beyond God's correcting hand?

Keep praying! No matter how impossible it seems. Even when your child wanders further and further away from the truth, keep praying. God is able to do the impossible ... even in Babylon!

Prayers for Wisdom, Knowledge, and Discernment

(More Scripture and prayers can be found at **http://www.susankmacias.com/unceasing**)

- Daniel 1:17, 20 (emphasis added): As for these four youths, *God gave them learning and skill* in all literature and wisdom, and Daniel had understanding in all visions and dreams.... And in *every matter of wisdom and understanding* about which the king inquired of them, he found them ten times better than all the magicians and enchanters that were in all his kingdom.
- I ask You to give my child wisdom and understanding, just like You gave these to Daniel and his friends. Our society feels more and more like Babylon, so I ask You to grant my child excellent discernment so he/she can thrive in these crazy times. May he/she understand that You are more important than anything the world offers.

- 1 Kings 4:29 (NKJV): And God gave Solomon wisdom and exceedingly great understanding, and largeness of heart like the sand on the seashore.

- Lord, I pray you would give my child exactly what You bestowed on Solomon: wisdom, understanding, and a large heart. Please use these gifts in his/her life to bring You glory and to grow Your kingdom.

- Psalm 111:10 (emphasis added): The *fear of the LORD is the beginning of wisdom*; all those who practice it have a good understanding. His praise endures forever!
- There is no wisdom without You, Lord. With You it begins, and through Your Spirit it flourishes. Please grow a healthy fear of You in my child and through that grow wisdom in him/her. May it result in enduring praise for You.

- Isaiah 11:2 (emphasis added): And the Spirit of the LORD shall rest upon him, *the Spirit of wisdom and understanding*, the Spirit of counsel and might, *the Spirit of knowledge* and the fear of the LORD.
- Holy Spirit, please rest on my child. Invade him/her with Your wisdom and understanding. Fill him/her with Your counsel and strength and cause knowledge and fear of the Lord to overflow his/her heart.

9

APPROVE WHAT IS EXCELLENT

Scripture:

So that you may *approve what is excellent*, and so be pure and blameless for the day of Christ.

(Philippians 1:10, emphasis added)

Prayer:

Lord, please help my child approve, discern, and understand what is excellent in Your eyes.

For six short months, we lived on the California coast in the quaint town of Monterey, California. After growing up visiting Texas beaches, the contrast was astonishingly beautiful.

Texas lies on the down-current side of the Mississippi River, which leaves a nice, muddy tint to the sand. California's coast contains a treasure trove of clean sand, and rocks with tide pools holding sea urchins and starfish. Taking my seven-, five-, and three-year-old boys to the beach brought every book we ever read about the ocean to life.

On one such trip, we discovered a secluded outlook, high on a cliff, offering uninterrupted vistas of the ocean below us. Dropping our picnic to one side, I stood spellbound. As waves crashed on the rocks below, sea otters and sea lions frolicked. Gulls called through the salt-scented air, and I spied the spout from a whale, far out to sea. What beauty!

The excited chatter of my sons crescendoed above the ocean sounds. I realized they must also be thrilled by this grand display of God's majesty! I turned from my reverie to join their happiness, only to discover the source of their excitement lay elsewhere.

All three searched through the dirt, and I heard one exclaim, "Look at all the bottle caps!"

"Wow! This is great! I bet I can find more than you!"

"I know—let's see who finds the most." With that, the Great Bottle Cap Hunt began. Even the three-year-old, with his close proximity to the ground, could compete with his older brothers in this contest.

Bottle caps? As I looked around, I realized I was not the first person to enjoy the seclusion of this spot. Apparently, a favorite drinking rendezvous for the locals, brightly colored caps from beer bottles of all varieties littered the ground.

What should my strategy be? Should I make them drop the caps and discuss the dangers of alcohol and underage drinking? No, at this point the caps had no connection to beer in my young sons' minds. Beer caps were just colorful, shiny, round treasures. The more they collected, the richer they would be.

Choosing the tactic of diversion, I exclaimed, "Boys, look! See the sea otters swimming down there? And how about that sea lion sunning on that rock? Wouldn't that be fun?"

Obediently, they glanced at the ocean and indulged their mom's enthusiasm. "That's great, Mom," said the oldest.

"Cool," added his brother. "And did you see these bottle caps, Mom?

Aren't they cool too? I bet I find the most!" And with that, his search resumed.

I felt astounded and fairly certain I had failed as a mother. Somewhere along the way, I obviously dropped the ball in training their appreciation of nature. They hunted through the dirt rather than viewing the splendid panorama, and chose bottle caps over grandeur.

I perched on a rock, stared out to sea, and sulked. As often happens, my Lord began gently working truth and enlightenment into my heart. Nagging questions began to overtake my frustration. How often had I traded the beauty of God's truth for some worthless trinket of momentary value? How often had Jesus wanted to lead me to heavenly beauty, but I refused to take my eyes off worldly treasure that was actually trash?

As I sat on my rock and allowed this conviction to work its way into my thinking, item after trivial item came to mind. These "bottle caps" were actually trash. I heard the words Jesus said to Martha in Luke 10:41; I was "worried and bothered about so many things," when there was really only one that was important.

Glancing at my sons rummaging in the dirt, I realized the most excellent thing I could do with them right then was hunt for bottle caps. Sulking certainly didn't represent Jesus well to them, and relationship trumps nature appreciation any day. I consoled myself that at least we were getting filthy in a beautiful setting.

As little boys, my sons were distracted by valueless bottle caps. But now, culture daily bombards my kids with cheap alternatives to truth. Multitudes of "un-excellent" options besiege the youth of today: social media, video gaming, continually streaming movies and shows, just to name a few. Smartphones deliver every imaginable diversion and sin right into the palm of their hands.

How will they recognize what holds eternal value when they are inundated with temporary pleasures? How can my kids ever be pure and blameless when they are surrounded by filth? The only possible solution requires heightened senses to detect what is excellent, and increased strength to run toward that.

But, the only place authentic discernment ever comes from is Jesus. Paul tells the Colossians that it is Christ "in whom are hidden all the treasures of wisdom and knowledge" (Colossians 2:3). So as I pray for my kids to approve what is excellent, I am asking Jesus to reveal the treasure of Himself to them. He not only displays to my kids the standard by which to measure true value, He also enables them to live like Him, even in the face of evil.

I Hit What I Aim At

Our families are not the first to live in evil times, where the struggle to approve excellence is a real battle.

Think back to the beginning. Adam and Eve lived in the perfect Garden of Eden. They enjoyed unmarred communion with each other and the animals and walked with the Lord in the cool of the evening. But somewhere, in the freedom of choice that God allowed in man, eating the ONLY thing they were denied seemed like an excellent idea. They traded intimate communion with God and life in a garden of abundance for a little piece of forbidden fruit. Ever since, mankind has held up junk and deemed it more worthwhile than the excellent ways of the Lord.

Fast-forward a few thousand years, and we find King David asking his people, "*How long will you love what is worthless and aim at deception?* But know that the Lord has set apart the godly man for Himself; The Lord hears when I call to Him" (Psalm 4:2b–3, NASB). Apparently the problem of loving valueless stuff is not a new issue. Of course, the same solution exists now, as then—calling out to the Lord. Prayer has always been the only answer.

Just like his people, King David struggled to keep his heart aimed at truth and goodness. A wise and rich monarch, David diligently fought to solidify his kingdom. He gathered materials so someday the Temple for the Lord could be built. He lived a life surrounded by opulence, and he had numerous wives and concubines. Yet, with all that, he still allowed his own lust to take his aim off the Lord's directives. He connived, schemed, and sinned so he could take Bathsheba, another man's wife, for himself.

When David confessed his sin and prayed for God's restoration in Psalm 51, he wrote, "Behold, You desire truth in the innermost being, and *in the hidden part You will make me know wisdom*" (Psalm 51:6, NASB, emphasis added). There is nothing new under the sun. Just like us, David needed truth, overflowing in wisdom, in order to approve excellence and aim for what was holy. When he didn't use that, lives were destroyed.

If Adam and Eve, living in perfection, and King David, living in abundance, struggled with keeping their focus directed toward excellence, why would we ever expect it not to be difficult for our kids?

The challenge to live a life approving excellence increases as the culture slides into greater rejection of God. We are not the first to live through such times. Known as the weeping prophet, Jeremiah grew up part of a priestly family in Judah at a time of both great idolatry and potential revival.

After a succession of evil kings, King Josiah reigned on Judah's throne for the first half of Jeremiah's life. Josiah tried to steer his wayward nation back to God. As a youth in those decisive times, Jeremiah felt God's call to be a prophet. He argued with the Lord that he was too young and did not know how to speak. But the Lord enables all He calls, and He did the same for Jeremiah.[27]

He served the Lord faithfully for years. As King Josiah made reforms, Jeremiah came alongside him to encourage and warn the people. However, after King Josiah died, the nation dove headlong into idolatry, even though Jeremiah continued to prophesy coming judgment. Not only did the people persist in walking away from the Lord, the last thing they desired was a pesky prophet reminding them of their sin. Jeremiah endured intense persecution for proclaiming the words of the Lord.

Early in Jeremiah's ministry, the Lord prepared him by explaining how devastating the coming judgment would be. He also gave Jeremiah a promise: "If you extract the precious from the worthless, you will become My spokesman" (Jeremiah 15:19b, NASB). Think about that. In the midst of evil and coming devastation, God promised there was still something precious. If Jeremiah had the eyes to see that, he would be able to proclaim the Lord to those around him.

Even if everyone around him pursued contemptible endeavors, Jeremiah could discern and chose to go after what mattered. He could approve what was excellent, because, regardless of how bad circumstances might become, the precious was still available to be found.

When we following the prayer in Philippians 1:10, we pray that the Lord will help our children discern what is excellent. We are asking Him to not only help our kids navigate the mess around them but also enable them to see and aim at the valuable, precious, and eternal.

Zig Ziglar said, "You hit what you aim at, and if you aim at nothing you will hit it every time."[28] I desire that my kids aim at truth, not deception. I want them to shoot for precious, not worthless. I crave that they target eternal, not temporal. I long with every fiber of my being that they aim for Jesus, and that they receive immeasurably more than they could ask or think (see Ephesians 3:20).

I pray that my kids will be like Jeremiah. I pray they will be able, like him, to extract the precious from the worthless and therefore be spokesmen for the Lord to their culture and generation.

It All Works Together

We live in upside-down times. What is good is called bad, and what is bad is called good. Isaiah warned the Israelites, "Woe to those who call evil good and good evil, who put darkness for light and light for darkness, who put bitter for sweet and sweet for bitter!" (Isaiah 5:20). This describes our day just as accurately as it did Isaiah's.

It might sound unreasonable or even impossible that our kids would desire holiness in the current atmosphere of our world. In the flesh it is! In fact, without Jesus it is impossible. This fact makes the prayers in Philippians 1:9–10 perfectly relevant for our day.

Because Paul first prays for abounding love in the Philippians' lives (see Philippians 1:9), I begin by praying for that as well. Supernatural love guided by discernment becomes a powerful force. It not only teaches its possessor what to love but also instructs him or her how to live out that love so that (see v. 10a) he understands what matters to the Lord.

Next, I pray that my kids will approve what is excellent, desire what is pure, and love what is holy. These actions grow directly as a result of a love that abounds "still more and more in real knowledge and discernment" (Philippians 1:9).

These kinds of love and wisdom cut through the illusions the world offers and lead a soul to value the Father's excellence. If my kids' love grows to overflowing proportions, guided by knowledge and discernment, they will naturally be drawn, magnetically, toward what is holy and pure.

This type of transformation results in a life that not only remains blameless and pure but also produces much fruit.

And that is why the prayer in Philippians 1:9–10 has become the cornerstone of my unceasing heart cry for my sons and daughters.

> Beware in your prayers, above everything else, of limiting God, not only by unbelief, but by fancying that you know what He can do. Expect unexpected things "above all that we ask or think."[29]
>
> — Andrew Murray

PRINCIPLE:

I can pray that the Lord would shape my children's understanding so they value what is excellent and eternal.

APPLICATION

Scripture: So that you may *approve what is excellent*, and so be pure and blameless for the day of Christ. (Philippians 1:10, emphasis added)

Prayer: Lord, please help my child approve, discern, and understand what is excellent in Your eyes.

- Pray that Jesus would give your child spiritual insight to see what is precious and what is worthless.

Like the story of my boys' distraction with the bottle caps, what worldly treasures distract you from what has eternal value?

Now think about your kids. What distractions do they struggle with?

You might want to write these down and post the list somewhere you will see it often. Pray for the Lord to help your kids to see His will in these areas.

Why do you think the fruit tempted Adam and Eve away from all of the perfect excellence around them?

Think about this question from the chapter: If Adam and Eve, living in perfection, and King David, living in abundance, struggled with keeping their focus directed toward excellence, how would we ever expect it not to be difficult for our kids?

How does this question challenge your thinking? How does it challenge you to pray?

Zig Ziglar said, "You hit what you aim at, and if you aim at nothing you will hit it every time." List some of your prayers for what you desire your children to aim at.

Why do you think it is important to pray for abounding love before we pray that they would approve what is excellent?

Prayers for Desiring Excellence

(More Scripture and prayers can be found at **http://www.susankmacias.com/unceasing**)

Praying the Lord will give a supernatural desire for excellence in our children is one of the best

- Romans 12:9 (NASB): Let love be without hypocrisy. Abhor what is evil; cling to what is good.
- I ask You to give my child a pure love, without a hint of hypocrisy. Give him/her a godly hate for what is evil. And give him/her the desire to hold onto what is good and perfect.

- Colossians 2:6–8: Therefore, as you received Christ Jesus the Lord, so walk in him, rooted and built up in him and established in the faith, just as you were taught, abounding in thanksgiving. See to it that no one takes you captive by philosophy and empty deceit, according to human tradition, according to the elemental spirits of the world, and not according to Christ.

- Jesus, please establish my child in faith in You. May the truth we have tried to teach be constantly on his/her mind. Protect my child from the empty, false philosophy that runs rampant in our world. Keep him/her free from deceit so he/she is able to be established in the faith.

- Colossians 1:9–11: And so, from the day we heard, we have not ceased to pray for you, asking that you may be filled with the knowledge of his will in all spiritual wisdom and understanding, so as to walk in a manner worthy of the Lord, fully pleasing to him: bearing fruit in every good work and increasing in the knowledge of God; being strengthened with all power, according to his glorious might, for all endurance and patience with joy.
- Lord, I ask You to help me to never cease praying for my child. No matter what I see, I want to persevere, believing in Your work. Please fill my child with knowledge, understanding, and spiritual wisdom. Enable him/her to walk in a way that pleases You, and may the wisdom You grant bear fruit for Your kingdom. Build my child's knowledge of You that he/she will have endurance and patience and power to do Your will.

- Proverbs 3:21–24: My son, do not lose sight of these—keep sound wisdom and discretion, and they will be life for your soul and adornment for your neck. Then you will walk on your way securely, and your foot will not stumble. If you lie down, you will not be afraid; when you lie down, your sleep will be sweet.
- Jesus, I ask You to keep sound wisdom and discretion right in front of my child's eyes. May he/she not be able to escape You! Please allow Your wisdom to breathe life into my child's soul, and let the results be so evident that others will see You in my child. As Your wisdom permeates his/her mind, please cause fear to flee and his/her sleep to be sweet.

10

FILLED WITH THE FRUIT OF RIGHTEOUSNESS

Scripture:

Filled with the fruit of righteousness that comes through Jesus Christ, to the glory and praise of God.

(Philippians 1:11)

Prayer:

Lord, please cause my children's lives to overflow with fruit for Your kingdom.

The summer of 2011 found South Texas in the third-worst drought ever recorded, and South Texas knows how to do drought. Because I have a knack of good timing, I had finally started my garden in the spring of 2011. For eight years I had dreamed and planned, but the year I finally began my agrarian adventures? The one a severe drought would reign over the entire growing season.

As I naively prepared the ground and planted seedlings in the spring, I had no idea the rain faucet would remain shut off for the next six months. I watered my plants every day through months of unrelenting heat that never saw the relief of cool rain. My efforts were rewarded with six tall, green tomato plants. With a sense of pride, I watched them grow in spite of difficult circumstances.

However, there was one problem. Although the plants looked healthy and even blossomed with the promise of delicious, vine-ripened tomatoes, very little fruit developed. And by very little, I mean four cherry tomatoes. Four.

If I factored in the cost of the plants, soil, and fertilizer, each tomato cost about $42.53. All the time, expense, and effort. So little fruit. Disappointed doesn't come close to describing how I felt.

One sultry afternoon while surveying the green, fruitless plants, I realized something. These seemingly healthy, yet totally fruitless plants perfectly pictured my greatest fear as a parent. What if my kids grew up to look good on the outside but never produced any fruit for the kingdom of God?

Raising good boys and girls who managed to remain neat and polite in public was never our goal. Our ultimate desire was to raise godly men and women. My vision had always been to raise warriors for the kingdom who would storm the gates of hell and proclaim the Word of the Lord. I admit to being a bit visionary and dramatic, but then again, why not dream big? If I raised kids who gained the whole world but lost their own souls, what would I have done?

God revealed an unsettling truth as I gazed at those deceptively green, falsely flourishing plants. As worthy as my goals for my kids were, I could not work fruit out of their lives any more than I could will tomatoes to grow on the vine. In my garden, I contributed watering, feeding, and weeding, necessary actions of any successful gardener. BUT, true fruit came from only one place—the mysterious life deep inside the vine.

These fruitless tomato plants suddenly symbolized many young people I knew, who, though raised in Christian homes, now pursued the hedonistic pleasures of the world. Some dressed smartly while doing so. Others touted higher education degrees. Their exteriors seemed successful, but I knew their parents grieved that inwardly they turned their backs to the Lord. Standing in my green, yet fruitless, garden, I prayed for those young men and women.

Hearing my own children inside the house refocused my pondering squarely back to these souls. My husband and I trained our children to say thank you and please. We compelled them to eat their vegetables. We took them to church and read them the Bible. We proactively *did* everything we could, and each one of those items mattered and contributed to their growth and development.

However.

(Don't you just hate the word *however*? It sounds like the falling of the other foot. It means that no matter how neatly and logically I work everything out, there is more to the equation.)

And never is there more to the equation than in this realm of parenting. My diligent parenting mattered, *however*, my kids' fruitfulness required more than my cultivation. I couldn't manufacture the mystery of the life of Christ in them.

Frankly, as a parent, not being able to force fruitfulness in my kids' lives felt irritating. But, since I could not cause spiritual rebirth in them, I also was released from the burden of the responsibility. Freed from that weight, I wondered what I *should* and *could* do.

Since my children's spiritual lives demanded the work of the Holy Spirit, I realized there was only one thing. There had ALWAYS been only one thing. Pray.

And there, in that sweltering, infertile garden, my burden to pray exploded into full force.

Gardeners of the Heart

Though released from the obligation to create the life of Jesus in my kids, I still had significant work to do. When I planted my garden, I tilled the soil, sowed seedlings, removed the weeds, and watered regularly. I researched the individual needs for different plants, because tomatoes and watermelon, for example, need different types of care. Diligence and responsiveness were required.

Parenting also involves intentional care. I must cultivate an environment that encourages growth. The variety in people is greater than that in plants. My children are crafted for the purposes the Lord specifically has for each of them. Their personalities, tendencies, passions, and strengths are designed by the Creator to fulfill their unique missions.

Of course, there is another element they are born with as well: a sin nature. It always disappointed me just a bit when my precious, near-perfect baby started exhibiting those selfish tendencies that indicated that this one, too, was inherently sinful.

At the intersection of our kid's abilities and his or her sin nature lies the conundrum of parenting. We try to encourage the strengths and gifts, while at the same time we attempt to curb the weaknesses and sins. We are not supposed to be engineers, tinkering with the design God hard-wired. Rather, we are trying to be gardeners: pulling weeds, fertilizing, pruning, and watering the gardens of our children's hearts. It is exactly as hard as it sounds.

Teaching to the agricultural communities of Judea, Jesus used gardening parables to demonstrate His kingdom. Remember the sower in Luke 8:5–9 who throws seed all over the place? Only some of the seed is successful, because, as every gardener knows, soil conditions matter. I can just imagine the farmers in the crowd, shaking their heads as Jesus tells the story. That sower was so foolish, wasting so much seed!

In the parable, some seed is thrown on the road, which is hard and dry. It is eaten by birds or trampled by passersby. The seed that lands on rocks withers from lack of moisture, and the seed thrown amongst thorns is choked out. However, the seed that falls into good soil produces a crop.

One day as I read this familiar parable, I suddenly saw myself in that sower. I was trying to sow as much seed as possible into my kids' lives. I read them Scripture, took them to church, exposed them to missionaries, and used every opportunity possible to get the seed in there. But this parable woke me up to the flaw in my approach. The seed was not the only ingredient. What was I doing about where the seed landed? If the soil of their hearts was hardened or filled with rocks or thorns, the seed could not flourish.

While in a garden I can easily remove rocks or thorns by pulling them out and hauling them off, the heart offers much greater challenges. How do I remove what I cannot see? Cultivating land necessitates physical work, whereas gardening the heart demands spiritual work. As handy as a "How To" checklist would be right now, I am sorry to say, there just isn't one. But I can tell you this, spiritual work requires spiritual tools.

The Bible is an extremely effective tool; however, if your child has rejected its authority, he may not listen. Christian fellowship can yield great power, but if your child has turned her back on the church she might avoid believers like the plague. Prayer is the only effective tool available that works whether your child participates or not. But prayer isn't easy.

I do not want to minimize this. Prayer equals hard labor. How hard? Breaking-up-packed-ground hard. Toting-rocks difficult. Pulling-up-thorns tough. You might emerge from this kind of prayer bruised and scratched. It could take a much longer time to prepare the soil than you estimated. And once the soil is prepared, the prayer doesn't stop. In fact, it has just begun.

When Paul asked the Romans to pray, he said, "I appeal to you, brothers, by our Lord Jesus Christ and by the love of the Spirit, to *strive together with me* in your prayers to God on my behalf" (Romans 15:30, emphasis added). Paul was requesting they partner with him in the task of praying.

That is what parents do—strive in prayer. We strive in prayer to prepare our kids' hearts. We work at prayer as seeds are sown. We struggle in prayer as weeds pop up and drought stunts growth. We endeavor in prayer as plants begin to grow. And we persevere in prayer as we detect the first potential fruit.

Every prayer I ever uttered aided the cultivation of my kids' hearts. But one truth remains, even with all that prayer, I cannot force my kids' lives to produce fruit. While spiritual fruit that builds the kingdom of God is the goal of my prayers, it can come only from Him.

I need to plant, water, and weed. But it has only ever been God who causes the growth and the fruit.

God Causes the Growth and the Fruit

Located right off the narrow strip of Greek land that separates the Ionian Sea and the Adriatic Sea, ancient Corinth served as a thoroughfare for not only merchants and sailors but also many varieties of travelers. Temple worship of various gods and goddesses proliferated. Let's just say it was an interesting city.

In this pagan environment, a new Christian church struggled. In the patchwork quilt of religious activity that surrounded them, the Christians toiled to define themselves. They began to quarrel over which church leader they identified with.

Maybe this was because of the influence of the other pagan residents of their city who would choose to associate with one god over another, claiming:

"I am of Poseidon."

"Well, I follow Aphrodite."

"The god Hermes has more power!"

Whatever the reason, the Corinthian church started choosing sides. Instead of humbly identifying with their need for Jesus, they lined up behind the teacher who had baptized them. And then, just like churches do today, they argued over petty rivalries and divisive preferences.

"I don't know why you think you are so superior, just because Peter baptized you. I am glad Apollos baptized me. His theology is much sounder."

"Well, I am not of Apollos! How can you listen to the music he uses? It is not of the Lord, I am sure. And his tunic is of the most shocking color. I am of Paul. His standards are much higher.

"You are both wrong, and I rejoice I am not like either of you. I am of Christ, because I am holy and particularly humble."

Even though the apostle Paul lived in Ephesus at the time, word of the Corinthians' bickering reached him. First, Paul scolded them for their self-centered attitudes, but next he added a gem of an explanation. While both he and Apollos ministered to this fledgling congregation, neither of them had ever been the source of their new life in Christ. Paul explains, "I planted, Apollos watered, *but God was causing the growth.* So then neither the one who plants nor the one who waters is anything, but *God who causes the growth*" (1 Corinthians 3:6–7, NASB).

This response resounds with life-breathing truth. As servants of God, both Paul and Apollos completed their important assignments to minister, teach, encourage, admonish, and preach Jesus to the Corinthians. Likewise, as parents we should faithfully complete our God-directed assignments. The work matters, and obeying God's commandments is ALWAYS mandatory.

However. (There's that word again!)

However, our work alone will never cause the seed of the Lord's truth to germinate and grow in the soil of our kids' hearts. The Lord of Creation, and He alone, causes life and growth. He started in Eden as He created Adam and Eve in His image. He began crafting a people for His name when He called Abram out from his home, sent him to Canaan, and gave him a new name, Abraham. He birthed generations of His people through Abraham and Sarah, after a lifetime of infertility. The prospect of a baby was so preposterous, Sarah laughed at the prophecy and so named their baby Isaac, which means "he laughs."

The Lord has been specializing in reversing barrenness ever since. Isaac and his wife, Rachel, were barren for twenty years before God gave them twins. The prophet Samuel was conceived only after his mother, Hannah, cried out to the Lord for a child. And John the Baptist was a miracle baby born to an elderly Zechariah and Elizabeth.

Do you have a child for whom you have lost hope? Does the barrenness in his or her life spawn hopelessness in your own heart? Do problems seem so insurmountable, resistance so strong, or rebellion so complete that eternal fruitfulness looks impossible?

Here is the bad news: It is impossible for you to fix your child.

Here is the good news: "Nothing is impossible with God" (Luke 1:37, NASB).

In His last dialogue with the disciples before His crucifixion, Jesus emphasized the necessity of His life in theirs when He said, "I am the vine; you are the branches. Whoever abides in me and I in him, he it is that bears much fruit, for apart from me you can do nothing" (John 15:5).

Apart from Jesus, we can do nothing, so it makes logical sense that our children have the same limitation. Apart from Jesus, barrenness is the only option. So, I ask Jesus to live in my kids, and for Him to plant them deep into Himself. That is the ONLY way they will be fruitful.

This truth is clearly displayed in Paul's prayer in Philippians 1:11. What is the source of the fruit for which he is praying? "Filled with the fruit of righteousness *that comes through Jesus Christ*, to the glory and praise of God" (Philippians 1:11, emphasis added).

Paul could not produce fruit in the churches to whom he wrote any more than we can produce fruit in our children. *However* (and this is a fabulous *however*), he PRAYED unceasingly for it because he knew a God who could. He asked the God who began life in a Garden, the Lord who produced streams in the desert, and the Savior who was the Vine from which spiritual life flows, to fill the lives of the Philippian believers with fruit of righteousness.

Praying for God to bring fruit is not only all we *can* do, it is all we *need* to do. So, parents, let's keep praying and praying for our kids' lives to be filled with the fruit that comes through Jesus.

Oh, what a privilege. And what a divine commission.

The righteous flourish like the palm tree and grow like a
cedar in Lebanon.
They are planted in the house of the Lord; they flourish
in the courts of our God.

— Psalm 92:12–13

PRINCIPLE:

I cannot cause spiritual growth in my children, but I can pray that the Lord will cause them to grow and be fruitful for His kingdom.

APPLICATION

Scripture: Filled with the fruit of righteousness that comes through Jesus Christ, to the glory and praise of God. (Philippians 1:11)

Prayer: Lord, please cause my children's lives to overflow with fruit for Your kingdom.

- Even if you don't see evidence of righteous fruit in your child's life right now, ask the Lord to multiply your child's growth so that fruit abounds in his or her life.

In this chapter I told you, "My vision had always been to raise warriors for the kingdom who would storm the gates of hell and proclaim the Word of the Lord." Think about your big vision for your children. Write it out below.

Do you struggle with feeling free from the responsibility of your child's spiritual life?

Does it help you experience freedom to realize that your child's spiritual life is God's job? Or does it scare you?

Consider the soil of your child's heart. What are the hard, packed places? Are there rocks and thorns?

The items you wrote above are specific issues to pray over. Don't give up, no matter how hopeless it seems. Remember, your confidence is in the Lord!

Meditate on the truths that fruit comes from Jesus and it is God who causes the growth. How does this make you feel? Spend a few moments praising the Lord who never stops working in our lives and our kids' lives.

As you pray, remember: Nothing is impossible with God (Luke 1:37, NASB).

Prayers for Fruitfulness

(More Scripture and prayers can be found at **http://www.susankmacias.com/unceasing**)

- Isaiah 32:15–16: Until the Spirit is poured upon us from on high, and the wilderness becomes a fruitful field, and the fruitful field is deemed a forest. Then justice will dwell in the wilderness, and righteousness abide in the fruitful field.
- Holy Spirit, please pour Yourself on us. May our family be a fruitful field. Through You, may justice and righteousness live in our home.

- Matthew 7:17–18: So, every healthy tree bears good fruit, but the diseased tree bears bad fruit. A healthy tree cannot bear bad fruit, nor can a diseased tree bear good fruit.
- Lord, please heal our diseases that we may produce good fruit for You. Bring health and life in and through my child that his/her life would produce an abundance of good fruit.

- John 15:4–5, 8: Abide in me, and I in you. As the branch

cannot bear fruit by itself, unless it abides in the vine, neither can you, unless you abide in me. I am the vine; you are the branches. Whoever abides in me and I in him, he it is that bears much fruit, for apart from me you can do nothing.... By this my Father is glorified, that you bear much fruit and so prove to be my disciples.

- Please, Jesus, live in my child, and allow my child to live in You. As Your branch, send Your life and Spirit into every fiber of my child's being that there would be much fruit and that the Father would be glorified. Please encourage and equip my child to be Your disciple.

- Galatians 5:22–23: But the fruit of the Spirit is love, joy, peace, patience, kindness, goodness, faithfulness, gentleness, self-control; against such things there is no law. (ESV)
- Thank You Jesus for the amazing fruit of Your Spirit. Without You, we would be lost. Please cause Your fruit to grow in my child's heart. May love, joy, and peace rule his/her spirit. Teach him/her to respond to others with patience, kindness, goodness, and gentleness. And lead him/her to a faithful life marked by self-control. May his/her heart be fertile ground for Your fruitful harvest.

PART V

DIVE IN!

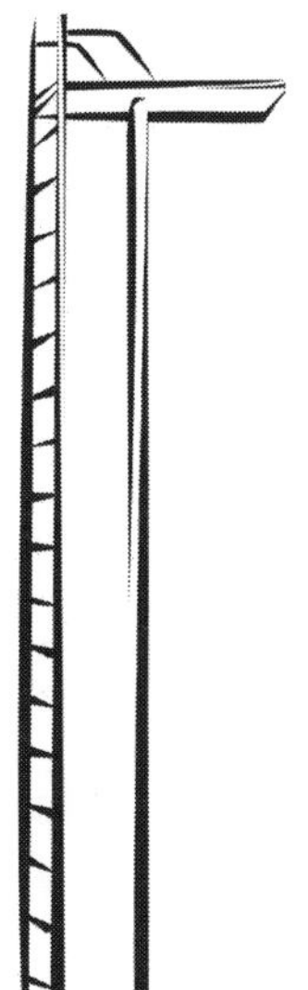

11

IT'S WAR BABY!

I give myself to prayer.
Psalm 109:4b

No man is greater than his prayer life.
...We have many organizers, but few agonizers;
many players and payers, few pray-ers;
many singers, few clingers;
lots of pastors, few wrestlers;
many fears, few tears;
much fashion, little passion;
many interferers, few intercessors;
many writers, but few fighters.
Failing here, we fail everywhere.[30]

— Leonard Ravenhill

So, what do you think?

Are you tired of striving, worrying, fretting, and nagging?

Are you exhausted from the constant stress and anxiety created by an unknown future?

Then it is time to pray!

The steps of prayer revealed in Philippians 1:3–11 are my antidote for my parental anguish. Now I hear warning sirens when fretting and worrying sneak into my heart. They alert me to areas I have taken back into my grubby, ineffective hands. I know I need to start the process back in Philippians 1:3 with the very first thing: thanksgiving.

But there are a few more prayer gems included in Philippians 1 that I use in particularly trying times. They have power to turn evil on its head, the biblical principle of redemption.

God's redemption begins in Genesis and repeats itself throughout the Bible. It climaxes at the point when Satan thought he had won, when Jesus died on the cross. Jesus takes that moment to redeem death, conquer hell, and achieve the ultimate victory.

C. S. Lewis paints a picture of redemption in *The Lion, The Witch, and The Wardrobe* when he records Aslan saying, "Death itself would start working backwards."[31]

As parents, we must remember that at no point is our child beyond hope or past redemption. No matter the outlook, we must keep praying to the great Redeemer.

Praying Anyway: For the Progress of the Gospel

I pray that the Lord's love abounds in my kids and that they live fruitful lives. But sometimes the answers to my prayers might look more like Paul's life, which, at the time, did not appear victorious.

As I have pointed out before, Paul understood tough situations like beatings, shipwreck, snake bite, and being imprisoned by the Romans. Even with all he endured, Paul repeatedly admonished and encouraged the Philippian church to rejoice.[32]

In every family's life, there are times when circumstances feel unredeemable. Crises can make it difficult to pray anything besides, "Help, Lord!" Even then, it remains vital to press past despair and fear into confidence and hope.

My kids have experienced some ugly junk: job loss, heartbreak, personal attacks, abandonment, illness, car accidents, business problems, learning difficulties, rebellion, just to name a few. Plus, there are all the consequences that result from their own bad decisions. I have never hurt as badly as when I hurt for my kids, or been as frustrated as when I watched them make stupid choices. However, to wallow in that pain or frustration cripples my prayer life.

Paul's response to his difficulties, found in Philippians 1, gives me a model to follow. When my kids experience or choose challenges from which I can't imagine any good, I take my cue on how to pray from these few verses in Philippians.

Paul redeems the worst of his problems with this declaration, "*my circumstances turned out for the greater progress of the gospel* ... most of the brethren, *trusting in the Lord because of my imprisonment*, have far more courage to speak the word of God without fear" (Philippians 1:12, 14, emphasis added). How like God. He takes the worst thing we can imagine and then uses that to advance the gospel.

This is the same principle Joseph told his brothers: "As for you, you meant evil against me, but *God meant it for good, to bring it about that many people should be kept alive*, as they are today" (Genesis 50:20, emphasis added).

God used Joseph's slavery to save Israel from starvation. He also used Paul's imprisonment to teach the church to have far more courage to speak and tell the world about Jesus. Talking of his own imprisonment, Paul could state that his own circumstances had "turned out for the greater progress of the gospel" (Philippians 1:12) because he proclaimed Christ to the Roman guard who watched him. What a clever method of missionary work!

Paul's response to his challenges both inspires and convicts me. He wrote this letter from a Roman prison, one in which he would eventually be condemned. Yet, he never asks for the Philippians to pray he would be released. Instead he states, "What then? *Only that in every way,* whether in pretense or in truth, *Christ is proclaimed*, and in that I rejoice. Yes, and I will rejoice" (Philippians 1:18, emphasis added).

I take my cue on how to pray for my kids from these verses. When my kids experience intense difficulties, I pray:

- Lord, please use this trial to the progress of your gospel. (v. 12)
- Jesus, I ask You to cause those watching this difficulty to be motivated, emboldened, and encouraged to speak Your Word without fear. (v. 14)
- Lord, in whatever way possible, please allow Christ to be proclaimed. (v. 18)

Behold, the Lord's hand is not shortened, that it cannot save, or his ear dull, that it cannot hear.

— Isaiah 59:1

A Little Full Disclosure

Do you feel inspired and ready to pray for your children like Paul prayed for the Philippians? I hope so. But, there are a few last points I need to clarify.

First of all, there are no "money-back guarantees" with prayer. The Lord is not on my timetable, and He may have vastly different futures planned for my kids than I do. God, being God, gets to do things His way, when He wants, for His purposes. Prayer is not obtaining a seat on the advisory committee to plan my kids' lives. Praying is more like breaking up the hard path, moving stones, pulling weeds, preparing good soil, and planting seed for God to do His best work.

Secondly, you and I may always be susceptible to anxiety and fear. Personally, the worry gene runs deep in my own DNA, with the women on my side of the family perfecting it to an art form. I KNOW how to worry and do it quite well! Too bad it is not an Olympic event. My prowess at worrying is why I need a solution so desperately.

When worry and fear alert me that I need a course correction, my very first step is thanksgiving. I offer thanks for everything that comes to mind, even the worst things my kids are going through.

Then, like a small child placing her hand in her daddy's hand, I begin to rest in my Abba's abilities to work out this situation in my child's life toward His plan. Instead of trying to steer Him in my direction, I slowly fall into step with my heavenly Father. I lean my head on His shoulder and ask Him to increase my kids' love so they love what He loves. I pray He causes their fruit to abound so He gets the praise! Though He rarely gives me assurances of exact answers, His peace envelopes my heart as anxiety recedes.

One last clarification, I must warn you, praying this way affects me as much as it affects my kids. As I began praying through Philippians 1:3–11, I realized how little I actually trusted the Lord to handle every single thing. Did I actually think He might run out of time or be too distracted by droughts and war on the other side of the planet to care for my little family?

I fight this battle still. But, no longer content to just sound like I hope in Jesus, I now desire to trust Him to my core. I am convicted every time I begin to reside in fear, or when I start to rely on myself and my efforts, rather than the working of the Holy Spirit.

> You find no difficulty in trusting the Lord with the management of the universe and all the outward creation, and can your case be any more complex or difficult than these, that you need to be anxious or troubled about His management of it?[33]
>
> — Hannah Whitall Smith

Now, as I face trials, any inner turmoil reveals a fear God might not take care of THIS problem. When I worry, I need to confess it quick. Then I can pray through these verses, redirect my focus, and return to my prayer platform of thanksgiving, joy, and corrected vision.

Using Philippians 1:3–11 as an outline for prayer also changes how I mother. Prior to immersing myself in these biblical truths, I labored under an anxiety-laden yoke. Even today, when there are problems, I often fall into the trap of worry, from which I tend to interact with a controlling spirit. My efforts to steer my kids out of trouble cause friction and conflict.

The bond of fellowship broken, I become less influential even while I work to get them back on course. They become more resistant, I try harder ... It is a vicious cycle.

If I want the relationship to improve, I must stop talking to my kids and start conversing with Jesus instead. "Come to me, all who labor and are heavy laden, and I will give you rest. Take my yoke upon you, and learn from me, for I am gentle and lowly in heart, and you will find rest for your souls. For my yoke is easy, and my burden is light" (Matthew 11:28–30). When I take the yoke Jesus offers to me, I reap the benefits of rest. This change in my perspective doesn't change my kids. It changes me.

When I stand alone, under the yoke of motherly love, dreams, and concerns, the weight crushes me. But, when I stand with Jesus, He takes the weight, ministers to my heart, and shows me ways to sacrificially love my family. I leave the responsibility for their earthly and eternal lives in His hands. I no longer try to control my children. The vicious cycle is broken, and as much as it depends on me, fellowship is restored.[34]

This does not mean I have become complacent as a mom. But now, instead of warring WITH my kids, I am warring FOR my kids. In an active, continual battle, I enter this fray with the enemy and fight for my kids every day.

Don't ever underestimate the eternal importance of your prayers for your children, even if they never know you are praying for them. Your prayers are your weapon. They are how you go on the offensive, charge the gates of hell, and fight for your children.

> We tend to use prayer as a last resort, but God wants it to be our first line of defense. We pray when there's nothing else we can do, but God wants us to pray before we do anything at all. Most of us would prefer, however, to spend our time doing something that will get immediate results. We don't want to wait for God to resolve matters in His good time because His idea of 'good time' is seldom in sync with ours.[35]
>
> — Oswald Chambers

Don't Stop!

"I love the Lord, because he has heard my voice and my pleas for mercy. Because he inclined his ear to me, therefore *I will call on him as long as I live.*" (Psalm 116:1–2, emphasis added)

The gauge to determine if I need to keep praying is if I am still breathing. As long as I am alive, I will pray for my children, even if I see no fruit from my labor. I will pray without ceasing.

"*Be patient*, therefore, brothers, until the coming of the Lord. *See how the farmer waits for the precious fruit of the earth, being patient about it*, until it receives the early and the late rains" (James 5:7, emphasis added).

The problem is, I have never been a patient person. But through the power of the Holy Spirit, when answers are slow in coming and all hope seems lost, I can recall Psalm 126:5: "Those who sow in tears shall reap with shouts of joy!" I patiently sow prayers, even if my heart is breaking, because I place hope in what Jesus will do.

Hope is required to pray unceasingly. Paul specifically prays for the Romans' hope in Romans 15:13: "May the God of hope fill you with all joy and peace in believing, so that by the power of the Holy Spirit you may abound in hope." Just look at this rich treasure:

- God IS hope. Because of that, hope is not something I must manufacture.
- Hope is God filling me with joy and peace. Once again, I don't manufacture the joy and peace. God fills me with these precious resources.
- Trust replaces despair as I REALLY believe the God of the universe loves my children and acts on their behalf.
- Notice the "*so that*." The result of the God of hope filling me with joy and peace: I will *abound* in hope! I will overflow with so much hope, I will have leftovers!

- In THAT hope, I keep praying, looking at the God of hope, not the sins (failings, struggles, hardships) of my child.

Just think, by the power of His Spirit, the God of hope cultivates the fruits of joy and peace, which prepare my heart for a flood of hope. That *hope fuels my perseverance to keep praying.*

I treasure the weight God lifts from my heart every time I pray with thanksgiving, joy, and vision. While resting in confidence of God's work in my kids' lives through His gospel and His grace, I pray their love abounds in wisdom so they can discern what matters. I pray this over and over again, asking God to guide their hearts to be blameless and pure, and that He would produce righteous fruit in them. And then I leave the production of the life-breathing, kingdom-building fruit in the hands of the One who can cause the growth.

Prayer is the single most important action you can take for your children.

Are you ready to start praying for your kids like Paul prayed for the Philippians? It is time to move from anxiety and fear to confidence and power. So, climb up on that scary platform, get into position, and bombard heaven with petitions for your children. You will conquer worry in yourself and invite God's power into your child as you pray unceasingly.

> When the devil sees a man or woman who **really believes in prayer**, who **knows how** to pray, and **who really does pray**, and, above all, when he sees a whole church on its face before God in prayer, he trembles as much as he ever did, for he knows that his day in that church or community is at an end.[36]
>
> R. A. Torrey

To pray without ceasing is not only Jesus's idea but also His command. The good news is that all unceasing prayers require are a starting point. Yours can be now.

Start praying for your children immediately, no matter how young or old they are, and never cease. It is the best thing you will ever do

---

EPILOGUE

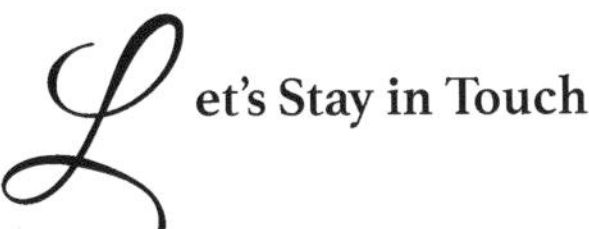

Let's Stay in Touch

I would love to hear how God uses prayer in your life as a parent.

I also want to stay in touch with you and offer you resources to aid your prayer life.

Join our Facebook page so we can help each other at: www.facebook.com/unceasingprayerforkids/

Just request to join and you can enter the conversation. Let's encourage each other in difficult times and pray for one another.

You can find more resources to encourage prayer at my blog: www.susankmacias.com/unceasing

There you can gain access to more scripture and prayers for the chapters of this book.

For all kinds of prayer encouragement go to my blog page: www.susankmacias.com/prayerguides

Enter the password: prayermatters

Feel free to download and use the prayer sheets there as often as you like. Check back periodically, as I add more through the year.

You can find me on the following social media platforms:

Facebook: www.facebook/susankmacias/

Instagram: Susan K Macias

Twitter: @SusanKMacias

ENDNOTES

[1] See Exodus 17:9–13.

[2] "30 Quotes That Will Help You Get Through the Day," Paul Sohn. November 7, 2013, accessed August 14, 2017. http://paulsohn.org/30-quotes-that-will-help-you-get-through-the-day/.

[3] "G4342 - proskartereō - Strong's Greek Lexicon (ESV)," *Blue Letter Bible,* accessed May 2, 2017, www.blueletterbible.org//lang/lexicon/lexicon.cfm?Strongs=G4342&t=ESV.

[4] See Colossians 4:12.

[5] See Hebrews 11:1.

[6] See Ephesians 3:20.

[7] "Prayer and Intercession Quotes (2)" Tentmaker Ministries, accessed August 14, 2017 www.tentmaker.org/Quotes/prayerquotes2.htm.

[8] Andrew Murray *Reaching Your World for Christ*, (New Kensington, PA: Whitaker House, 1997).

[9] Merlin Carothers, *Prison to Praise* (Escondido, CA: Merlin R. Carothers, 1992), 91-92.

[10] Francis Chan and Danae Yankoski, *Crazy Love: Overwhelmed by a Relentless God* (Colorado Springs, CO: David C Cook, 2015), 42.

[11] Tim Keller, "Worry and Bitterness," Daily Keller. Tim Clark, December 27 2014, accessed March 30, 2015 http://dailykeller.com/714/.

[12] See Romans 8:28.

[13] NET Bible.

[14] See Ephesians 3:20.

[15] "G2842 - koinōnia - Strong's Greek Lexicon (ESV)," *Blue Letter Bible*, Accessed May 3, 2017, www.blueletterbible.org//lang/lexicon/lexicon.cfm?Strongs=G2842&t=ESV.

[16] Oswald Chambers *My Utmost for His Highest: Selections for the Year* (Uhrichsville, OH: Barbour, 1991), 272.

[17] Genesis 15:1b.

[18] Genesis 15:3

[19] Genesis 15:5, NASB.

[20] Paul David Tripp, Twitter post, November 22, 2014, 6:38 a.m., https://twitter.com/PaulTripp.

[21] "G5426 - phroneō - Strong's Greek Lexicon (ESV)," *Blue Letter Bible*, accessed May 3, 2017, www.blueletterbible.org//lang/lexicon/lexicon.cfm?Strongs=G5426&t=ESV.

[22] See Romans 8:26–27.

[23] J. I. Packer *Knowing God* (Downers Grove, IL: InterVarsity, 1973), 226.

[24] Dietrich Bonhoeffer, *The Cost of Discipleship* (New York: Collier, 1963), 183.

[25] Associated Press "American David Boudia Wins Gold," ESPN, ESPN Internet Ventures, August 11, 2012, accessed May 3, 2017, www.espn.com/olympics/summer/2012/diving/story/_/id/8258951/2012-london-olympics-david-boudia-wins-1st-diving-gold-us-2000.

[26] "G4052 - perisseuō - Strong's Greek Lexicon (NASB)," *Blue Letter Bible*, accessed May 3, 2017, www.blueletterbible.org//lang/lexicon/lexicon.cfm?Strongs=G4052&t=NASB.

[27] See Jeremiah 1:4–11.

[28] "Top 30 Zig Ziglar Quotes," Hear It First. June 7, 2014, accessed August 14, 2017, www.hearitfirst.com/news/top-30-zig-ziglar-quotes.

[29] "Great Quotes On Prayer," Eternal Perspective Ministries. Randy Alcorn, March 28, 2009, accessed May 3, 2017, www.epm.org/resources/2009/Mar/28/great-quotes-prayer/.

[30] Leonard Ravenhill, *When Revival Tarries* (Ada, MI: Bethany House, 1959).

[31] C. S. Lewis and Pauline Baynes, *The Lion, the Witch and the Wardrobe* (New York: Harper Collins, 1978), 163.

[32] See Philippians 2:18; 3:1; 4:4.

[33] Hannah Whitall Smith, *The Christian's Secret of a Happy Life* (Boston, MA: Charles Cullis, 1885), 73.

[34] See Romans 12:18.

[35] "30 Quotes That Will Help You Get Through the Day," Paul Sohn. November 7, 2013, accessed August 14, 2017. http://paulsohn.org/30-quotes-that-will-help-you-get-through-the-day/.

[36] Melanie Redd. "6 Great Reasons For Us to Pray," Valerie Murray.

June 23, 2017, Accessed August 14, 2017. www.valeriemurray.com/6-great-reasons-for-us-to-pray/.

ABOUT THE AUTHOR

Susan Macias is a writer, speaker, and teacher whose goal is to build strength and courage in women to faithfully follow Jesus, serve their families, and build the Kingdom. Her work has been published in national and regional magazines, and she writes weekly on her blog. Married to her college sweetheart Nathan for 33 years, they have homeschooled their seven children since 1993. You can find Susan at her blog, susankmacias.com.

www.susankmacias.com
susan@susankmacias.com

Made in the USA
Middletown, DE
21 December 2017